TAKING BACK THE GOSPEL

MOVING WITH LOVE TO FORWARD THE GREAT COMMISSION

NANCY GOLDEN

All Scripture quotations, unless otherwise indicated, are taken from the Holy Bible, New International Version®, NIV®. Copyright ©1973, 1978, 1984, 2011 by Biblica, Inc.™ Used by permission of Zondervan. All rights reserved worldwide. www.zondervan.com The "NIV" and "New International Version" are trademarks registered in the United States Patent and Trademark Office by Biblica, Inc.™

"I Love to Tell the Story" (1866); Author: A. Kate Hankey, (1869); Refrain: William G. Fischer, in the public domain.

For information or inquiries, contact Nancy Golden at
nancy@goldencrossranch.com

Library of Congress Control Number: 2024904833

Published by Golden Cross Ranch LLC
Carrollton, Texas U.S.A.

Cover Photo by Pronoia / Adobe Stock License

Cover Design by Naomi Golden Creative LLC

To my husband, Phil Golden, my beloved and my best friend. I thank God every day for bringing us together and for the wonderful man of God, husband, and father that you are. Thank you, Phil, for always being my support and encouragement and teaching me how to love Jesus better through your own example.

To Joshua Golden, my son and chief encourager, to Jay Morgan, who inspires me and makes me laugh, and to Katherine Deans Evanson, who has shown me Christ all of our lives.

CONTENTS

FOREWORD

When a friend or church leader encourages you to share your faith, does it send chills down your spine? You know Christ has called you to obey the Great Commission, but you feel inept, scared, and frankly out of your league. If you have ever felt this way, Nancy Golden's book, Taking Back the Gospel, is just for you.

In its pages you'll discover that Jesus never intended the Great Commission to be left only in the hands of the professional clergy or well-spoken theologians, quite the contrary; Nancy contends the Great Commission is an appeal for every Christian to reach out through the power of the Holy Spirit and in the love of Christ to what she calls your personal Jerusalem.

But how are we to reach out? How are we to approach the Great Commission? Through loving people, this is how we take back the Gospel. In one of the more telling lines of the book, Nancy writes, Have fun—give yourself permission to enjoy yourself—and your friends will too. Evangelism is easy, just love your neighbor.

What a refreshing approach to evangelism. Just love your neighbor. No pressure, no canned techniques, rather we are encouraged to be the person that only we can be, do that thing that only we can do, trusting all the while that God is using us as His ministers of reconciliation to a lost and dying world.

Nancy isn't asking us to push the unbeliever into a corner until we force a sinner's prayer out of them, rather following the style of Jesus who told his disciples just before sending them out on their first evangelistic endeavor to have the wisdom of a snake and the gentleness of a dove, Nancy exhorts us to be flexible and let the Holy Spirit be the one in control.

Nancy wrote her book with the local church in mind. The book would be perfect for a Sunday school class, Wednesday night Bible study, or a church-wide evangelism seminar. The study questions at the end of each chapter are great discussion starters and her chapter on *The Fundamentals* will equip all of your church members with effective modes of sharing the Gospel. Her favorite illustration on a napkin will no doubt be a handy tool for many.

Taking Back the Gospel is a book for everyone who longs to bring the good news of Jesus to a lost and dying world. I am grateful for a book that once again stirs our hearts to love our neighbor and declares that our greatest privilege is to be Christ's ambassador.

Chad Burton
Senior Pastor
Living Word Global Church

PREFACE

I don't know about your house, but Saturday at the Golden house is chore day. It's the day we do all of the things we don't have time to do during the week. Our then seven-year-old son Joshua had one chore he particularly hated. It was his job to change the sheets on his bed on Saturday mornings.

The specific day that I am recalling started out as a typical Saturday morning. I was sitting at the kitchen table working on homework. Phil was working on "guy stuff" in the garage. Joshua was in his room, supposedly changing his sheets. He had been in his room quite a while, but this was not unusual. Joshua not only hated to change the sheets on his bed; he took as long as possible, making it a long, drawn-out, and painful process. Eventually, he came out of his room and stood by my chair.

"Mommy, I have to talk to you." "Okay," I replied. I put my pen down and turned to face him. "What is it, Josh?"

Josh was holding a big gold coin in his hand, one of those gold dollars that had come out in recent years. Josh held it towards me. "Mommy, I swallowed this," he informed me. "It got stuck in my throat but I finally got it out."

My heart dropped in my chest. I can't describe what I felt at that moment ... the feeling of shocked horror at what could have happened. My son could have choked to death in the next room, while I calmly sat at our kitchen table, working on my homework.

My son had been in our home—in his own room. I had not felt a need to check on him because I knew he was as safe as he could possibly be. Or so I thought...I have to tell you, I got down on knees numerous times over the next few weeks, thanking God for saving my son.

That Saturday could have turned out much differently, and I praise God that it turned out the way it did. Joshua was fine. And after seeing his mother burst into tears, he became a little wiser about putting things in his mouth.

There are many reasons to evangelize, which we will explore in Chapter One, but certainly the above story is a very compelling one. The words of the psalmist from Psalm 103:15-16, "As for man, his days are like grass, he flourishes like a flower of the field; the wind blows over it and it is gone, and its place remembers it no more" speak to the fragility of life.

In view of life being so fragile, what could be more important than our eternal life?

A young man from our church's youth group was coming home from a soccer game when he died in an automobile accident. Josh Hernandez was an incredible youth who loved Jesus and lived for Him every day. As painful as it was to receive the news that this precious young man had gone to be with the Lord, we could celebrate that those were not empty words in a phrase often used at such times—because we knew with as much certainty as one can have of another person, that Josh Hernandez had indeed gone to be with his Lord, since his life had been a reflection of his passionate love for Jesus.

To quote Pastor Dan Dean, "Most people think they are physical beings with a spiritual presence, but in reality, we are spiritual beings with a temporary physical presence." God made us for eternity; Ecclesiastes 3:11 tells us, "He has made everything beautiful in its time. He has also set eternity in the hearts of men; yet they cannot fathom what God has done from beginning to end."

It is this very fragility of life that should serve as a motivating force for evangelism. What a blessing it is to know that for Josh Hernandez it is not truly "goodbye," but rather, "see you again in heaven someday," because someone took the time to invest in his life and show him Jesus Christ as Lord and Savior; God calls each of us to the same task.

In 2 Corinthians 5:20, we learn that we are described as Christ's ambassadors. While an important part of our goal is to love people in the Name of Jesus (The Second Greatest Commandment), our ultimate goal is to help bring them into their own personal relationship with God that leads to eternal life (The Great Commission). Get ready for an exciting journey as we seek God's heart for evangelism!

The Second Greatest Commandment is found in Matthew 22:36-40.

"Teacher, which is the greatest commandment in the Law?"

Jesus replied: "'Love the Lord your God with all your heart and with all your soul and with all your mind.' This is the first and greatest commandment. And the second is like it: 'Love your neighbor as yourself.' All the Law and the Prophets hang on these two commandments."

The Great Commission
is found in Matthew 28:16-20.

Then the eleven disciples went to Galilee, to the mountain where Jesus had told them to go. When they saw him, they worshiped him; but some doubted. Then Jesus came to them and said, "All authority in heaven and on earth has been given to me. Therefore go and make disciples of all nations, baptizing them in the name of the Father and of the Son and of the Holy Spirit, and teaching them to obey everything I have commanded you. And surely I am with you always, to the very end of the age."

1

WHY EVANGELISM?

Reason One: Because the Bible Tells Me So

The first step in committing to any endeavor is to understand why it is desirable to do so. As Christians, an important starting point is to seek God's will in His revelation to us through Scripture. Tim Dearborn writes, "It is insufficient to proclaim that the Church of God has a mission in the world. Rather, *the God of mission has a Church in the world.*"[1] Henry T. Blackaby and Avery T. Willis also write, "He has never been willing that any should perish. God's mission is to glorify His name, to establish His kingdom and to reconcile the world to Himself."[2]

God is on a mission and always has been. He desires our worship because He is a relational God; He delights in our love and in the love He bestows on us.[3] God makes his mission clear from the beginning and Genesis 12:1-3 declares His plan. God's universal intent to call ALL nations to Him is made through Abraham,[4] and accordingly, through Abraham's seed:

The Lord had said to Abram, "Go from your country, your people and your father's household to the land I will show you.

"I will make you into a great nation,

and I will bless you;

I will make your name great,

and you will be a blessing.

I will bless those who bless you,

and whoever curses you I will curse;

and all peoples on earth

will be blessed through you."

To take this a step further and make it relevant to Christians today, we need to look at Galatians 3:29, which works in tandem with the truth of Genesis 12:1-3: "If you belong to Christ, then you are Abraham's seed, and heirs according to the promise."[5]

Paul's declaration brings with it the responsibility of that inheritance; it is through us as believers that the promise is carried out, by going to the families of the earth with the Gospel.[6] From the very beginning, God has declared His redemptive plan for all peoples and He has made us partners in His plan!

Scripture further instructs us in the Great Commission as to how we are to approach the task in Matthew 28:18-20,

Then Jesus came to them and said, "All authority in heaven and on earth has been given to me. Therefore go and make disciples of all nations, baptizing them in the name of the Father and of the Son and of the Holy Spirit, and teaching them to obey everything I have commanded you. And surely I am with you always, to the very end of the age."

Reason Two: In Preparation
for Our Lord's Return

George Eldon Ladd comments that Matthew 24:14 is the "clearest statement in God's Word about the time of our Lord's coming,"[7] wherein Jesus tells us, "And this gospel of the kingdom will be preached in the whole world as a testimony to all nations, and then the end will come."

This statement from our Lord creates urgency for world evangelism in us, as Christians who yearn for all to come to know Jesus as Savior and to see Christ return. It shows the nature of God, who from the beginning has declared His desire to be worshiped by all nations; also expressed in Psalm 96, especially in verses 2-3: "Sing to the LORD, praise his name; proclaim his salvation day after day. Declare his glory among the nations, his marvelous deeds among all peoples."[8]

Scripture is clear: God intends to include all peoples in their worship of Him, and Jesus will not return until the Gospel has been brought to all nations. The basis for preaching the Gospel is unmistakable. The anticipated return of Jesus gives urgency to the evangelistic mission; His certain return fosters hope, encouraging Christians to live with a spiritual presence rather than an earthly one.[9]

Reason Three: Being On Mission to a World
That Desperately Needs Jesus

THE APOSTLE PAUL's heart affected his strategy. In Acts 17:16 we learn, "While Paul was waiting for them in Athens, he was greatly distressed to see that the city was full of idols." Rather than being impressed by the Athenian architecture, his heart is broken by what he sees. He recognizes their desperate need to know Christ.[10]

Paul's mission theology is driven by his need to share the salvation of the Gospel message with lost people. This need is not only in regards to their eternal destination, but out of a Christ-like compassion for others, so that Jesus can be their anchor during the storms of life.

I would not want to contemplate traveling this earthly journey with its accompanying struggles that are the result of a broken world, without Him by my side. We should want the comfort found in the Psalms for everyone. Psalm 18:1-2 tells us God is both our strength and our salvation,

> I love you, Lord, my strength.
>> The Lord is my rock, my fortress and my deliverer;
>> my God is my rock, in whom I take refuge,
>> my shield and the horn of my salvation, my stronghold.

Psalm 46:1-3 gives us assurance that even when our world falls apart, God is our refuge and ever-present help.

> God is our refuge and strength,
>> an ever-present help in trouble.
>> Therefore we will not fear, though the earth give way
>> and the mountains fall into the heart of the sea,
>> though its waters roar and foam
>> and the mountains quake with their surging.

To participate in mission work is to participate in the kingdom of God. What an incredible privilege we have to be on mission with our Savior. Blackaby and Willis beautifully express what it means to be *On Mission with Jesus,*

In this partnership, you will become involved in His mission to reconcile a lost world to God. To be related to Christ is to be on mission with Him. You cannot be in relationship with Jesus and not be on mission. Jesus said, "As the Father has sent me, I am sending you" (John 20:21)... Nothing could be more precious than to follow God on mission in the same way that Jesus did.[11]

We should never lose sight of the fact that evangelism brings us into the reality of the very nature of God and His mission for humanity to be reconciled to Him through His Son Jesus Christ.

Reason Four: The Confidence of Being Reunited With Our Loved Ones in Heaven

PEOPLE COMING to Christ should be of utmost importance, especially when the alternative of hell is such a disturbing reality. On a very personal level, if we want the assurance of seeing those we love in heaven, it is incumbent upon us to help them to meet Jesus. While this task may seem overwhelming to some, it must be remembered that it is the Holy Spirit who ultimately draws people to Christ.

We do whatever we can to facilitate a conversion as the Holy Spirit leads, but the final result is never our responsibility. A Scripture comes to mind here for those of you who may be discouraged in this regard: Nothing is too hard for the LORD! (Ref Genesis 18:14).

I had the amazing privilege of witnessing to my mother who is Jewish. She had grown up going to a synagogue and as an adult, she had retained her Jewish identity. My brother and I benefited from a wonderful childhood in which we were raised as Christians on my father's side, but also got to experience our Jewish roots.

Sadly, on multiple occasions, my mother had experienced discrimination by Christians because of her Jewish heritage. In my limited human perspective, becoming a disciple of Christ seemed very far away for her.

But God had a different perspective and it was through the leading of the Holy Spirit that I had the incredible joy of sharing about Jesus with my mother during Thanksgiving one year. At the age of 87, she accepted the Messiah Jesus Christ as her Lord and Savior. It doesn't get any more personal, or joyful, than that! You can read more about it in Appendix A, "A Jewish Contextualization of the Gospel."

We can indeed celebrate the truth of 1 Corinthians 15:55-57,

"'Where, O death, is your victory? Where, O death, is your sting?' The sting of death is sin, and the power of sin is the law. But thanks be to God! He gives us the victory through our Lord Jesus Christ."

QUESTIONS FOR DISCUSSION

1. What prevents us from reaching out to our unbelieving family members, friends and neighbors when we understand what the alternative is for those who do not know Jesus as Lord and Savior?
2. Which reason for evangelism resonates most with you? Why do you think that is?
3. What do you think is significant about Psalm 67 in regards to evangelism?
4. What do the Great Commission and the Second Greatest Commandment have in common?

5. Can you think of any other verses that support God's plan for evangelism?

6. After reading Appendix A, can you think of anyone in your own sphere of influence that may be at a similar place to where my mother was, perhaps even referring to themselves as a Christian but not fully comprehending the Gospel message? What are some non-threatening things you can do to help them move forward into a genuine relationship with Christ?

2

WHERE TO EVANGELIZE?

The Big Picture

God's plan for reaching the world with the Gospel message is two-fold: The Great Commission commands Christians not only to witness to distant places, but in their own countries, cities, and streets as well. In Acts 1:8, Jesus tells his disciples, "But you will receive power when the Holy Spirit comes on you; and you will be my witnesses in Jerusalem, and in all Judea and Samaria, and to the ends of the earth."

After His words, Jesus ascends into heaven, leaving his disciples with a mission, the same one we share today: through the power of the Holy Spirit, we are to bring the Gospel to a world that desperately needs a Savior. We can gain a better understanding of the scope of His words if we are willing to make the following analogy:

We start with Jerusalem, the city that was the center of Jewish worship and was the stage for much of the New Testament. We could say that Jerusalem is representative of our own city, where we live and conduct our daily activities.

The next two places mentioned in the passage are Judea and Samaria. Samaria is North of Judea and South of Galilee. In keeping with our analogy, Judea and Samaria could be considered what we think of as North America—still within our immediate geographical sphere with regards to the rest of the world.

And finally, Scripture tells us to witness to the "ends of the earth," meaning the entire world. Understanding the scriptural mandate to reach our community is an important step. This does not mean that we should not bring the good news overseas, but it does mean that witnessing in our own communities is also part of God's plan.

Our Jerusalem

The focus of our time together in this book will be on evangelizing in *Our Jerusalem,* that is, in our own community. Many if not most of the principles we will be learning apply "to the ends of the earth," but we will be addressing the mission field in our own backyard.

The people in our community make up a diverse population and can be divided into two segments. First, the United States was founded as a Christian nation under God, but people have become enmeshed in a secular culture that no longer subscribes to biblical truths. This is a unique time when the United States has distinct Christian roots but must now be evangelized because people have either revised or rejected the Gospel.[12]

Second, we have a large immigrant community that consists of people from around the world. International students in our schools and universities are included in this segment.

Your Personal Jerusalem

Let's take this a bit further and identify who is in your

Jerusalem. The checker whose line you always gravitate toward in Walmart is in your Jerusalem. The folks that serve you at Mom's Diner are in your Jerusalem. The garage door repairman who arrives to fix your garage door is in your Jerusalem. So is the neighbor behind the alley who only calls when she needs something. And the neighbors that moved in next door who don't speak English very well, but have children that go to school with yours.

Your sister that you only talk to every month or two is in your Jerusalem; your nephew who is struggling with a drug addiction is as well. The lonely widower who walks down the street with his wife's dog every evening and the person sitting next to you in church are in your Jerusalem.

There are a lot of models on evangelism and one that can help us here is called the "concentric circles of concern," by Oscar Thompson.[13]

Thompson's model starts from the center, with the relationships that we each have in our own Jerusalem. The relationships grow more distant with each circle, ending in Person X, which we can take to mean strangers. What is important to realize here is that each circle represents someone in your direct area of influence. The potential impact you can have in each relationship is up to you—to reach out to your own Jerusalem.

> *What is God's plan to deal with this darkened, decaying world? His plan is us! There is no one else. It isn't going to be given to anyone else. It doesn't belong to famous evangelists. They'll never touch the people you touch. It doesn't belong to great preachers, or people on the radio or television, or people who write books. It belongs to all of us. This is God's divine plan. ---John MacArthur[14]*

But There Are So Many! How Do I Know Who God Wants Me to Reach Out To?

THIS IS the true joy of evangelism—that it is not dependent on you, but that the Holy Spirit will use you to accomplish His purposes. As Christ followers, we should strive to show the love of Christ in every situation we find ourselves—and that is a witness in and of itself. But when do you take it to the next level and personalize the relationship? That also is up to the Holy Spirit.

Evangelism is a venture to be approached prayerfully and with discernment of the Holy Spirit's leading. It is not through our own efforts that people are reached; it is the love of Christ that is at work transforming us so that God can use us with the end result being the work of the Holy Spirit. With this in mind, it is also important to realize that the Holy Spirit often works on short notice—any encounter might turn into kingdom work!

APPENDIX B "THAT'S NOT A PROSTITUTE" gives additional insight on witnessing to others that just might rock your world and make you examine some attitudes you may not realize you have —like it did for me.

QUESTIONS FOR DISCUSSION

1. What has your attitude been towards the people who serve you (waitress in a restaurant, gas station attendant, repairman)? If you are paying for a service, does this affect your attitude? Should it?
2. I'll never forget the time I was visiting a church that I had not been to before and it came time to shake hands and greet the person next to me. I turned to

my neighbor and held out my hand with a smile. She grabbed my hand and then turned back to the friend she was sitting with, her back angled towards me, as she shook my hand vigorously while continuing to converse with her friend. How would this have made you feel? How might this have affected a person who came to church that day hurting or seeking Christ?

3. Think about Thompson's "concentric circles of concern" and how they apply to your own Jerusalem. Fill in whoever the Holy Spirit brings to mind as you consider each relationship:

- Immediate Family
- Relatives
- Close Friends
- Neighbors/Co-workers
- Acquaintances
- Strangers

4. After reading Appendix B, can you think of anyone in your Jerusalem that you may have been looking at from an earthly viewpoint? Try to view that person through the same lens that Jesus does. How does doing that change your attitude towards that person?

3

THE ROLE OF CULTURE IN EVANGELISM

What is Culture Anyway?

There are many definitions of culture which can be confusing to navigate. For our discussion purposes, we will be using the one by Paul Hiebert, which states that culture is "the more or less integrated systems of *learned* ideas, feelings, and values encoded in patterns of behavior, signs and products created and shared by a community of people."[15]

A related term that is also important for our study is "worldview." According to *Introducing World Missions* by Scott Moreau, Gary Corwin, and Gary McGee, "Worldview essentially describes the way people understand and interpret the world around them."[16]

A person's worldview results in that person making judgments on the people around them and their behavior, which can have a long-term impact on future communication. By being culturally sensitive, we can prevent misunderstandings that would otherwise hinder our witness.[17]

As we described in the previous chapter, our community is made up of a diverse population in need of evangelization, which includes Americans who have become secularized, as well as people who have emigrated here from other countries and are in need of Christ. For the sake of our study, we will be combining these segments as it is my contention that EVERY effort towards evangelism is cross-cultural, because at some level we bring our baggage with us wherever we go.

That baggage includes where and with whom we experienced our childhood and our formative years. Thus, if I am witnessing to a middle-aged white American woman, I still may have cultural bridges to cross. My father died when I was fifteen, which caused our family to become disrupted during the turbulent teenage years, and she may have come from a relatively stable two-parent home. She might have grown up as an only child, whereas I grew up with a big brother.

Our experiences define us culturally in ways we are often unaware of on a conscious level. They help to form real attitudes that do exist, whether we understand how they got there or not. That is why I especially value the statement regarding the learning of culture, "This takes place broadly by a process of absorption from the *social environment,* especially *in the home,*"[18] which by extension recognizes that every evangelistic endeavor is a cross-cultural one.

Because of this, we will be looking at ways to build bridges in our community to different groups with the understanding that each outreach experience is unique, but that there are some principles we can apply universally in order to begin building those bridges.

****Important Concept****

Before we go any further, I want to address those of you who are feeling rather intimidated at the moment, now that we have pointed out the cultural divisions that should be considered when formulating a strategy for evangelism.

For those of you who are saying to yourselves, "How will I ever be able to relate to someone else different from me?" I would like to emphasize that you do not have to have shared experiences to evangelize. But you do have to have sensitivity towards the other person's worldview, which is affected by his culture.

We are often guilty of Matthew 5:46-47,

> If you love those who love you, what reward will you get? Are not even the tax collectors doing that? And if you greet only your own brother, what are you doing more than others? Do not even pagans do that?

It is harder to reach out to those who are different from us culturally—it takes us out of our comfort zones and it takes time. I like to imagine how God must smile when we do "the hard thing" to glorify Him. You can do this! The only essential prerequisite is a desire to share the love of Christ with others. It is through the power of the Holy Spirit that the task is accomplished!

Contextualization

WHEN WE ARE TALKING about contextualizing the Gospel, we are talking about communicating it in a way that our audience can understand. First, we need to identify the audience. It doesn't matter if they are Arab, Chinese, or the American nonbeliever who went to VBS as a kid, professes a belief in God, but has his value system anchored in secular culture. To effectively witness to any of these audiences, contextualization is necessary.

Our goal is to share the Gospel in a way that does not compromise Scripture, yet allows the audience to identify with the Gospel story through the lens of their own worldview.

The Monkey and the Fish

A MONKEY, sitting safely on his island during a flood, notices a fish struggling mightily against the water. The monkey says to himself, "I will go save the fish." So at considerable risk to himself, he climbs a tree that has a branch overhanging the water where the fish is swimming against the tide. Making his way carefully down the branch, he reaches into the water and manages to grab the fish.

He scampers back down the tree and carefully places the fish on the sand, feeling intense pleasure that he has saved the fish from the flood. The fish flops around in agitation for a few moments, but eventually falls into a peaceful sleep.[19]

We can easily conclude from this story that even when we have the best intentions, if we don't try to see each other through the other person's worldview, misunderstandings can result.

This is also true in our efforts to share the Gospel, as illustrated in David J. Hesselgrave's article, "The Role of Culture in Communication"; he writes of a village in Africa that has a custom when people come to visit, they will call out rather than knock on the door. The reasoning is that thieves knock on the door to see if anyone is home, and if no one answers, they feel free to go inside and rob the home. So a friend calls out with their voice, but a thief knocks.

Just imagine the translation problem with Revelation 3:20, "Here I am! I stand at the door and **knock**. If anyone hears my voice and opens the door, I will come in and eat with him, and he with me."[20] This brings home the importance of the role that contextualization can play!

Our best example in Scripture is that of the Apostle Paul who wrote in 1 Corinthians 9:20-22,

> To the Jews I became like a Jew, to win the Jews. To those under the law I became like one under the law (though I myself am not under the law),-so as to win those under the law. To those not having the law I became like one not having the law (though I am not free from God's law but am under Christ's law), so as to win those not having the law. To the weak I became weak, to win the weak. I have become all things to all men so that by all possible means I might save some.

In Acts 17, Paul's task is to relate to the men of Athens in such a way that they can understand the Gospel message. He is now ministering to the Gentiles, so the Old Testament Scriptures that Peter had been using to witness to the Jews with such great effectiveness no longer apply.

Paul understands this and alters his presentation accordingly. The Greeks of Athens value philosophy, so he emulates their methods of dialogue and quotes their own philosophers to illustrate the points he wants to make.

This is what we mean by contextualization: bringing the Gospel message in a way that your audience can understand it. If Paul had quoted prophecy from the Torah, it would not have meant anything to his audience. By quoting the Greeks' own philosophers, Paul built a bridge that brought comprehension to his audience.

We have introduced some new ideas regarding culture and contextualization for you to think about. Don't worry, we will be discussing these further and giving you the tools you will need to be comfortable in incorporating these ideas into your own personalized evangelism strategy! You can get a more personal view of cross-cultural evangelism to the immigrants in our community by reading Appendix C, "The Mission Field in Our Own Backyard."

QUESTIONS FOR DISCUSSION

1. What are some distinctive elements of American culture?
2. What are some distinctive elements of the culture in your own home?
3. What are some cultural values that can affect how a person views the church?
4. Can you think of some experiences in your own life that have helped to shape your own world view?
5. What did you think about the monkey and the fish? Can you think of a time when you were the monkey? Can you think of a time when you were the fish?
6. What do you think might be some of the important differences to consider when attempting to befriend someone from another country?
7. Consider our example of Revelation 3:20 regarding the role of culture in communication. How could you translate the verse for its African audience while staying true to its original meaning? Can you think of another example of taking a biblical text and preserving its inner meaning while transposing it into your own culture?
8. After reading Appendix C, can you identify any immigrants in your Jerusalem? What would be a good first step in reaching out to the immigrant community in your own neighborhood?

4

TRADITIONAL APPROACHES TO EVANGELISM

Overview

E vangelism has been a primary occupation of the church since New Testament times. The Book of Acts shows us that believers witnessed the Gospel as a part of the Christian life, rather than seeing it as an activity reserved for planned occasions. Acts 8:4, "Those who had been scattered preached the word wherever they went."

We have a distinct message and a mandate from our Lord to present it, but He doesn't give us an exact method. I believe this is because the method that is most effective depends both on the messenger and the recipient of the message, and the Holy Spirit has an active role in the presentation.

There are many different methods for evangelism; we are going explore an approach that combines elements of several methods in order to help you to create an effective strategy that is so comfortable that it becomes a natural part of you.

What it will require from you is a willingness to be open to the leading of the Holy Spirit and a commitment to explore different methods, as well as trying some on until you find what works best for you. Our efforts must be Spirit-led, but preparation is also our responsibility as we mature in our faith.

I also want to emphasize that as much as we hope to share Christ with our friends, we are never to regard them as a "project." They are people we care about who are in need of Christ, just as we all are, and it is the Holy Spirit who ultimately does the work.

We can and should be intentional, but we cannot expect to have a scheduled agenda. The Holy Spirit may choose to use us at anytime and we need to stay open to His leading.

Traditional Approaches

Evangelism Tracts

MANY OF YOU have heard of the *Roman Road* or the *Four Spiritual Laws*. These are often printed on a tract to hand out to people with minimal commitment on your part; the people you give them to can take the information and go.

While these tracts do share the Gospel message, they are typically inadequate in moving a person to accept Jesus as their Lord and Savior by themselves. You can put them in your evangelism toolbox, but probably only to assist you when explaining the Gospel, after you have already invested time in building a relationship with whomever you are witnessing to.

Direct Single Encounter Approach

SHARE JESUS Without Fear by William Fay[21] is a fairly assertive approach primarily developed for one-time encounters. It provides questions that are designed to get a conversation started with anyone, including strangers, which can lead to "The Five Share Jesus Questions" that explore how close the person is to God, starting with "Do you have any kind of spiritual beliefs?" If the person you are conversing with responds positively to the initial questions, then it will lead to sharing key Scriptures that are very similar to the *Roman Road.*

After walking the person through the Scriptures, five additional commitment questions are asked such as, "Do you want forgiveness of sins?" If taken positively, these questions will lead to praying the *Sinner's Prayer.* While this method has been used very successfully, it is not an approach that I personally favor. However, Fay makes a good point in that you might be led by the Holy Spirit into a one-time encounter that could impact someone's eternity, if not immediately, then perhaps by setting the stage for a future commitment. Paul writes in 1 Corinthians 3:6, "I planted the seed, Apollos watered it, but God made it grow."

I would definitely take the parts that help you in your own personal approach. Gaining a familiarity with Fay's method has helped me to be more confident in my own evangelistic endeavors by giving me more tools for my toolbox. I actually used the Scripture format from Fay's book when witnessing to my mother on the day she accepted Christ.

Personal Testimony

EVERYONE HAS A STORY. Personal testimonies are the stories of how people have come to know Christ as their Lord and Savior —they consist of what brought them to that point in their life. A testimony can also be a story about how God has helped a person through a difficult period or experience.

Some stories are rather dramatic, while others sound quite ordinary. Both extremes and everything in between are great testimonies, because there will always be other people who can relate to your personal story in ways that only the Holy Spirit can foresee.

I knew of a beautiful Christian lady who was an exemplary mother, wife, and church volunteer. I met her for breakfast one morning and she confided in me that she was disappointed in her personal testimony because it was boring. She said it couldn't have the same impact as the ones that told of a person coming to Christ after immense personal struggle.

I looked at this precious woman of God who was a light to everyone in our church and outside of its walls and could scarcely believe my ears. I reassured her that what she termed a boring testimony was much to be desired! It gives people hope for their own families that being faithful and obedient are values that can be embraced by their own children—so that they too, can become strong, loving Christian adults. I told her I would have traded for her personal testimony any time!

God could very well use our personal testimonies either as inspiration or as a way to reach others who are on similar paths, as we see in 2 Corinthians 1:3-4,

> Praise be to the God and Father of our Lord Jesus Christ, the Father of compassion and the God of all comfort, who comforts us in all our troubles, so that we can comfort those in any trouble with the comfort we ourselves receive from God.

Even after we become Christians, we have struggles, yet we have full confidence that God is with us every step of the way. Sharing a story about an illness you may have had to walk through, the loss of someone important to you, or any of the millions of issues that must be dealt with here on earth in a fallen world, are all ways to touch someone else on a level that could help them on their journey if they are already a Christian, or help someone who is seeking God to come closer towards a relationship with Him.

These are great reasons why every Christian should have a personal testimony ready. In 1 Peter 3:15 we are told, "Always be prepared to give an answer to everyone who asks you to give the reason for the hope that you have." By reflecting on your personal testimony and preparing it in advance, it will come easily to mind when needed.

Adopting a Consistently Evangelistic Lifestyle

REMEMBER our discussion about who is in our Jerusalem? How can we be a witness for Jesus to the grocery store checker at Walmart or our waitress at Mom's Diner? By casting off our entitlement attitudes that are rampant in this country, and adopting an attitude of friendliness and gratefulness wherever we go!

No opportunity is too small to make someone feel cared about. We are representing Christ in everything we say and do. Most waiters and waitresses will tell you that they hate working on Sundays because of the church crowds who are very demanding and tip very poorly. What does this say about the Body of Christ?

We can all work towards reversing this image by taking time to be thoughtful and courteous to our servers. A great start is simply inquiring about how they are doing and meaning it. Greet the people who cross your path for whatever reason and ask how their day is going. If they feel led to share, listen with empathy. People respond when you show that you are really interested and care about what they are saying, regardless of your location.

In the past six months I have had an opportunity to pray with a checker at Walmart, with a lady that was also waiting for her husband when I was waiting for Phil in a doctor's office, with the plumber that was fixing a leak in our home, with the gentleman that was handling the finance paperwork for my car at a local dealership, and with the lady that I had just interviewed with for a job!

Each had expressed a specific concern and very much wanted me to pray for them when I offered. You can have full confidence that God will use you when you start looking for opportunities to show His love to those around you.

Not everyone is comfortable praying with other people spontaneously and that is perfectly fine. Being a sympathetic listener and offering a few words of encouragement have the same effect.

Once you start being open to these types of opportunities, you may be surprised at how aware you become of the people around you and the Holy Spirit's leading that allows you to be a witness for the Gospel. Matthew 5:13-16,

> You are the salt of the earth. But if the salt loses its saltiness, how can it be made salty again? It is no longer good for anything, except to be thrown out and trampled by men. "You are the light of the world. A city on a hill cannot be hidden. Neither do people light a lamp and put it under a bowl. Instead they put it on its stand, and it gives light to everyone in the house. In the same way, let your light shine before men, that they may see your good deeds and praise your Father in heaven.

Service Evangelism: Individuals and Small Groups

Individual acts of service evangelism are well defined by Steve Sjogren, the author of *Conspiracy of Kindness*. He writes, "loving deeds done by unassuming Christians convince more people of the love of God than all the words in the world."[22]

Dallas Willard, University of Southern California School of Philosophy, comments on Sjogren's method, "An outbreak of kindness is about the only thing that can make the gospel credible in a world that thinks it has already heard it all. Let's show the world, frozen over with fear and resentment, what First Corinthians 13 love can accomplish. Real kindness is a supernatural reality of the cross and the resurrection. It breaks the grip of evil wherever it goes."[23]

Sjogren also quotes Mother Theresa, "True acts of love go before God forever as worship to Him," and he further comments, "Instead of just telling the gospel, we are *bringing* the gospel to people. Our society expects to be preached at by enthusiastic Christians. It is almost shocking to unbelievers when we break that expectation by offering simple, practical demonstrations of God's love."[24]

This type of evangelism is a great way to show the love of Christ because anyone can do simple acts of kindness. Sjogren is careful to emphasize that servant evangelism equals deeds of love plus words of love plus adequate time.[25]

This method can be seen more as a way to open a door or cause a person to start thinking about God in response to the loving act that was offered. Sjogren refers to this as focusing on planting, not harvesting.[26] And who knows, that one act may be all that is needed to bring someone into the family of God who has already been considering it!

Evangelism of this type can be done by individuals, but it is also a great fit for small groups. The possibilities are endless and can be done with minimal time and financial commitments. Sjogren's book lists many ideas to get you started, including doing a totally free car wash, a soft drink give away, Christmas gift wrapping, and leaf raking.[27]

Servant evangelism projects provide wonderful opportunities to answer the question that will be inevitably asked, "Why are you really doing this?" to which you can respond, "Because if Jesus was physically walking the earth today, He would be showing you the love of God in practical ways."[28]

One small group that I was a part of decided to do a project every three months. We visited a nursing home and sang Christmas Carols with the residents on one occasion. On another occasion we cooked a meal for the residents of a hotel in our area that consisted of displaced people from Hurricane Katrina. The lives you touch with the love of Jesus by doing simple acts of kindness bring so many blessings in the smiles you see in return!

Don't Forget Our Own Church Family

EVANGELISM MAY VERY WELL INDEED BEGIN AT home, our church home that is. An important thing to remember is that the person sitting next to you on Sunday will probably fall into one of five categories:

1. They are a committed Christian and are participating in the community of Christ.
2. They are a nominal Christian who usually attends church on Sunday but doesn't think much about spiritual things during the week.
3. They have never truly committed themselves to Christ, although they give the appearance they have. They are attending either from external expectations or habit.
4. They are what many call a "seeker." They have come

to realize they have a hole that nothing has been able to fill and are searching for answers.
5. They are in crisis and hurting, and are seeking someone to respond to their needs.

A kind word, an offer to pray, or an invitation to lunch can go a long way. Exchange phone numbers or email addresses, and follow up with a call. "Hi, it was so good to see you at church the other day. I just thought I'd give you a call and see how you are doing ..." If you learn of a real need, then you can also take a step (with their permission) and inform other members of your church family so that everyone can share in the response to help; needs can't be met by the Body of Christ if they are not made aware of them.

It could be something as simple as someone needing a ride to a doctor's appointment. I was at a church once that had a great ministry which was coordinated by a member of the congregation, called "Dr. Taxi." Whenever someone needed a ride to a doctor appointment (typically our older members), they would call Dr. Taxi and a volunteer would be assigned. What a great ministry that goes a long way in meeting physical needs yet requires minimal commitment, since one person handles the scheduling logistics and the assignments are rotated among church volunteers!

A Word About Long Term Evangelistic Ministries

EVANGELISTIC MINISTRIES that require an extended commitment warrant a brief mention here. The possibilities for reaching the community with the love of Christ through ongoing church ministries specifically geared towards community outreach are important, but due to the utilization of church resources including time, finances, and people that these ministries typically require, they are beyond the scope of this book.

This should not serve to discourage anyone that feels led to start such a ministry, as it does fall within the realm of servant evangelism, but its organizational nature and the amount of resources needed require a much more extensive treatment. An example that I have been a part of in the past is an ESL (English as a Second Language) Ministry.

Single Parent ministries are also a great way to meet real needs with the love of Christ. From my experience, these types of ministries are wonderful ways to build relationships that can help the people being served to come to know Jesus and commit their lives to Him.

All of these approaches have one thing in common, the importance of making people feel welcome and accepted. To learn how we as Christians sometimes fail in this and the harm that it causes so that we can guard against it, read about an incident that happened in Appendix D and reflect on how it could have been prevented.

QUESTIONS FOR DISCUSSION

1. What are some of the advantages and disadvantages of using evangelism tracts?
2. What are some of the advantages and disadvantages of using the direct single encounter approach?
3. What are some obstacles to adopting a consistently evangelistic life-style?
4. What are some ways that you can get involved with servant evangelism? List some ideas you could do individually and with a small group that would be feasible to try in the next month. What do you like

about this method and what do you think are
disadvantages to this approach?

5. Did it surprise you to see your own church family
   included as an outreach for evangelism? What can
   you do personally to step up to the plate and
   evangelize in your church?

6. HOMEWORK: Write your personal testimony. It
   shouldn't take more than a couple of minutes to
   share, so try to be both concise and impactful. If you
   are reading this book as part of an evangelism class,
   we will be sharing our testimonies with each other in
   our next class. Otherwise, make a personal
   commitment to share your testimony with someone
   in the coming week.

7. After reading Appendix D, take a moment to reflect
   on how open you are with others. Taking Elmer's
   example of the Bible study his wife attended, what
   could the participants have done to make his wife
   feel welcome?

5

CREATING A RELATIONAL APPROACH TO EVANGELISM THAT IS RIGHT FOR YOU

My Personal Favorite: Relational Evangelism

Quoting Scripture will probably not bring anyone to faith, unless it has been accompanied by a loving relationship. Our response to both the Second Greatest Commandment and the Great Commission should be in building those relationships.

Keith E. Swartley observes that Christians believe love and care for people are synonymous with bringing them the Gospel message and when our friends see that we truly love them, they also see the love of Christ demonstrated, softening their hearts to be receptive to the Holy Spirit's message.[29]

David Wheeler writes, "Genuine Christian love, as demonstrated through genuine believers, is the most attractive component in effective evangelism."[30]

A Brief Definition of Post-Modernity and its Effect on Evangelism

WE HAVE SEEN a shift of thinking in society across the late twentieth century and into the twenty-first that affects our view of truth. Truth is no longer an absolute; instead, it is defined by individuals according to their own personal experiences. This attitude is characteristic of what has been dubbed post-modernity, a phrase that attempts to capture the cultural shift that has occurred in our society subsequent to the period of modernity, which was based in rationale and logic.

Will McRaney simplifies for us what this means in regards to evangelism, "Those who have a postmodern paradigm place a higher value on experiences and relationships."[31] I mention this because "post-modernity" has been a topic in evangelistic circles as a hot button that must be considered in any evangelistic strategy. I would argue that this is not just a phenomenon accorded to post-moderns, but for moderns or anyone that you are attempting to evangelize. Relationship will be valued almost every time over rational arguments by anyone at any time.

But we still need to keep in mind the other aspect of post-modernity because it has become epidemic in our secularized society: the relativism that has been accorded truth. Pluralism (all religions are paths to God) and universalism (any way you choose to live your spiritual life is okay since it is your truth) have replaced the absolute truth of the Gospel (John 14:6, "Jesus answered, 'I am the way and the truth and the life. No one comes to the Father except through me'") in American culture. These attitudes are challenges that you may need to address as you grow in your relationships with your friends.

But I'll tell you a secret – I don't worry too much about that stuff. I focus on loving people, and that is enough to overcome any of these obstacles.

The saying, "People don't care about how much you know, they just want to know how much you care," is the most important factor in any attempt to build relationships. Once trust is achieved based on a relationship built through love, people will have an open heart to what you have to say.

Evangelism is Easy, Just Obey
The Second Greatest Commandment

RATHER THAN OFFERING a canned technique for you to employ, which probably won't do you much good when you get into a real life situation since life seldom follows a preplanned script, I am going to offer you some ways to simply love your neighbor. Relational evangelism is exactly that—building relationships.

As you start building bridges with the people that God has put on your heart to share His Gospel with, opportunities will eventually arise for spiritual conversations. But it is God's time-table, not yours, and the most important things are to be prayerful and to depend on the Holy Spirit to give you discernment, as you should be doing in every other area of your life.

Suggestions for Loving Your Neighbor

People Not Projects

GO into this endeavor looking at people through the same lens that our Savior does—each made in God's image and so precious that God sent His beloved Son from heaven to reconcile them to Himself. Each person is unique and specially made by our Creator. A project is something that you do; evangelism is something that God does through you.

Don't Set Any Agendas

I went to the home of a friend of mine to have lunch. On more than one occasion, our conversation has turned to spiritual things, and I even had the opportunity to share with her the Gospel in Café Brazil (See *Gospel Illustration on a Napkin* in Chapter Six).

On this particular occasion, I arrived at her home at noon as planned, and the visit lasted six hours! We talked about many different topics, including our families and different careers that might be a good fit for her. She remembered what we had discussed in Café Brazil and had more questions. I went into greater detail about the Holy Spirit, the need for repentance and how sanctification works. Each visit has been building on the last as she continues to seek answers.

I am not saying that you must devote this much time to every effort towards building friendships, but that there may be an occasion when that is the right thing to do. I didn't have any predetermined topics or a time-table in mind and we had a wonderful time. As a result, my friend is very receptive to talking about religious topics and our relationship continues to grow.

Forcing an agenda in these situations will only serve to prevent the intimacy of friendship that develops when you just let things move naturally. This doesn't mean you can't have a general plan; it just means to be flexible and let the Holy Spirit be the One ultimately in control.

You may not touch on a spiritual topic during your encounter, but it may be a great opportunity to reflect the love of Christ to the person you are witnessing to in a tangible way, and that may serve to open the heart of your friend to the Gospel in the future.

Be Yourself

There are multiple reasons for this. God made you with your unique gifts and abilities. Being yourself takes advantage of your God-given talents. It is also so much easier to be real than to try to maintain a façade. People may not know you are phony at first, but they will eventually figure it out.

By being yourself, you are living your own personal testimony and God will use that to His glory. So just chill out and don't worry about trying to be someone you aren't.

Accept People

This doesn't mean condoning sinful behavior, but it does mean loving people where they are at, just like Jesus did for us.

Notice the response Jesus gives in Matthew 9:11-13,

> When the Pharisees saw this, they asked his disciples, "Why does your teacher eat with tax collectors and 'sinners'?"
>
> On hearing this, Jesus said, "It is not the healthy who need a doctor, but the sick. But go and learn what this means: 'I desire mercy, not sacrifice.' For I have not come to call the righteous, but sinners."

Do A Little Homework

If you know you are going to be attempting to build a relationship with someone in your sphere of influence and it is possible, try to find out a little bit about them. If they are from another country, learn how to say hello to them in their native language, or find out about their holidays and offer them a holiday greeting at the appropriate time.

If someone in their family has a special accomplishment like a child winning a soccer game, make sure and congratulate them. If someone has a hobby, have some questions ready that show you are interested in what they are doing. Taking interest in what they are interested in will go a long way in showing them that you care.

When Explaining Something – Try to Do It In a Way That Your Audience Can Relate To

This goes back to what we talked about in Chapter Three regarding contextualization and our example of Paul in Athens. We want to make sure that we are communicating to people in ways that they can understand. Find out as much as you politely can about the person you are building a relationship with. Being a good listener as well as being observant will help you to understand your audience.

In this way you can effectively communicate with them and not only prevent misunderstandings, but with the leading of the Holy Spirit, you will be able to touch their hearts. He may use you to speak to them in ways that would often not be possible for them if you were communicating in an unfamiliar context.

Allow Your Witness to Unfold Naturally

This one goes back to agendas. To set a goal of converting a person in a certain time frame is very arrogant—it assumes that the responsibility for the conversion is yours rather than the Holy Spirit's. Bathe your efforts in prayer. Allow the Holy Spirit to guide you, and just enjoy the incredible privilege that God is using you to show someone His love.

Don't be Argumentative or Defensive.
Check Your Ego At The Door.

Your job is neither to argue your case nor to defend your faith, it is simply to share it. Arguing only makes your attempt at evangelism an uncomfortable confrontation. Defending your faith is unnecessary, because the truth will always lead to Jesus. You just need to realize that it takes time and that it is God's job, not yours. He has very big shoulders and can handle whatever anyone throws at Him!

Be A Good Listener

Worth saying again—be a good listener. If you want to build a relationship with someone, listening to them touches a basic human desire.

I heard on the radio about a mall in California where some entrepreneurs have set up shop offering professional listening services. For twenty-five bucks, you can have the undivided attention of someone who will listen to every word you say. They will not offer any comments or advice in response; their function is solely to listen. From what I understand, there are lines of people waiting their turn.

Listening is important. It allows you to get to know someone on an intimate level and it meets a fundamental need.

Have Fun

This one is essential—give yourself permission to enjoy yourself—and your friends will too. Having a Bible study as an evangelism strategy won't be terribly effective, but a barbeque and volleyball game will!

I taught ESL (English as a Second Language) for the Adult

Education Center here in Carrollton. My students were adults who had immigrated here from around the world. Most of them were extremely nervous their first day of class and I taught the beginning level, so they spoke very little or no English. My first job was to make them feel comfortable and wanted. No one would be able to learn well if they were uncomfortable.

By having class parties, allowing plenty of time for breaks, and making the class enjoyable by having games and interactive learning, we grew into a family over the course of the semester. We had class parties both at school and in our home. I took my students on picnics and to ride my horse. Eventually, the students started coming to our home for a bilingual Bible study. But it all started with FUN!

Drinking alcohol is a topic that is not usually discussed in church circles regarding evangelism because of the conviction that many people have that drinking alcohol is sinful, especially since the damaging effects of alcohol to individuals and families have been well documented. Appendix E has been included to confront and stimulate your thought on this matter because it explores real world scenarios that can definitely have an effect on your witness.

QUESTIONS FOR DISCUSSION

1. What does it mean to engage in relational evangelism?
2. How does relational evangelism compare to the methods Jesus used in the New Testament? What are some specific examples?
3. What are some advantages and disadvantages to this method?
4. What are some obstacles to building relationships?

5. How can you overcome the obstacles that were mentioned in responding to Question 4?

6. Which suggestions do you find comfortable and which ones do you struggle with and why? Pick one and brainstorm how you can be more effective in implementing it in your own personal evangelism strategy.

7. Appendix E is obviously based on a controversial subject among Christians. Take some time to explore this topic and share your feelings and experiences that have shaped your opinions. How would you respond to the three scenarios that are presented?

8. If you are reading this book as part of an evangelism class, take some class time for everyone to share their personal testimonies with the class. If you run out of class time, you can continue with personal testimonies during the next class. If you are not part of a class and have not already done so, make sure and find someone that you can share your personal testimony with.

6

THE FUNDAMENTALS

B efore we cover the basics, I am going to quote Carl Medearis, who is well known in missionary circles in the Middle East and writes about the advantage we have as Christians,

> We know the Creator. We're friends with the King. We know where truth is found. We know what brings life and what gives life and where eternal life resides. While others are explaining and defending various 'isms' and 'ologies,' we're simply pointing people to our Friend. The one who uncovers and disarms. Who leads people right to himself. The beginning and the end of the story.[32]

I think Medearis is right on the mark—we have a personal relationship with the Lord of the universe and He is leading people to Himself. What a privilege that He chooses us to participate in the process!

Understanding That It Is A Process

While there are essential elements to the Gospel message that must be communicated correctly according to Scripture and properly understood and accepted in order for a person to come into a saving relationship with Jesus, we need to understand that this doesn't necessarily (and most likely won't) happen in one sitting.

Even if you do manage to communicate all of the important elements, it may have to be done multiple times before true comprehension and acceptance occur, if at all. I am returning to Paul's gardening analogy—we may be setting the stage for a future commitment.

Do not feel bad if the person requests that you change the topic—matters of the heart can't be forced. If the person is not ready, your job is to let the Holy Spirit complete the work on His time-table. Do your best to return to the point of trust and friendship that you had reached in your relationship before bringing up the Gospel.

You may be pleasantly surprised at a later time when your friend wants to continue exploring spiritual questions; you may have given them a lot to think about at one time and they simply needed time to absorb it.

Communicating the Essential Elements of the Christian Faith

In order to share our faith, we need to understand the essential elements that constitute what it means to be a Christian. While part of our goal is to love people in the Name of Jesus (The Second Greatest Commandment), our ultimate goal is to help bring them into their own personal relationship with God that leads to eternal life (The Great Commission).

We don't have one without the other, so we don't want to be so busy building relationships that we forget what our ultimate purpose is. What this means is that you present an active witness when the Holy Spirit opens an opportunity for you to do so—so you need to be ready and understand the information that He is guiding you to present.

This does not mean you need to be a seminary-trained Bible scholar or a Christian for several years. New Christians often offer the most effective witness because they have a level of excitement that those of us who have been around for awhile may have lost. Indeed, new Christians often bring revival to old ones!

An Important Thing to Keep in Mind

You probably won't know all of the answers to everything you are asked and that is perfectly okay! There is nothing wrong with the response, "I don't know," as long as it is accompanied by, "but I will find out for you."

Also remember that there are lots of opinions as to what should be communicated and there are many resources for you to use in determining the answer to this question for yourself through the guidance of the Holy Spirit, including your pastor and Christian mentors, as well as the myriad of books that are available on evangelism.

Always be sure that you consider the credibility of your source when you are doing your research, as we are warned in Matthew 7:15, "Watch out for false prophets. They come to you in sheep's clothing, but inwardly they are ferocious wolves."

My Favorite Gospel Illustration on a Napkin

EVERY PERSON IS UNIQUE, so how you witness to them will be unique as well. When it comes time to start explaining the Gospel to someone, you will need to discern how much they understand, and how much explanation they will need for concepts that may be new to them.

FIRST, I draw a chasm with stick figures on one side. I usually make one with curly hair like me, and the others with hair like those I am with, commenting about what I am doing just to keep it fun and interesting.

. . .

NEXT, I discuss how we are separated from God by sin. I usually spend a couple of minutes talking about sin and how we are all born with a sinful nature. I mention that Scripture tells us in Romans 3:23 "for all have sinned and fall short of the glory of God," and to further illustrate this point, I ask them if anyone had to teach them how to lie.[33]

I usually get a little smile in response on that one and I say, "Let me give you an example. When you took a cookie you weren't supposed to when you were little and your Mom asked you if you took it and you said no, did anyone have to teach you how to do that?" I have always gotten the same response: the person shakes their head—no.

I go on to explain that God is on the other side of the chasm (I usually mention that the sun does not represent God, that I just draw it to show that where God is, it is a good place since sunshine is usually a positive image). I explain that God is Holy and because of that, He cannot be in the presence of sin. So we have a big problem since we have already determined we are sinners; we cannot enter His presence (cross the chasm) on our own.

.   .   .

Now I say, "But here's the Good News! God provided for us a way to come into His presence and be with Him through His Son Jesus Christ." I draw the cross at this point to bridge the chasm and then I continue, "By dying on the cross, Jesus took on the entire burden of all of our sins so that we could become righteous, enabling us to cross the chasm through His sacrifice. It is through His resurrection that we have eternal life."[34]

Now if you think about this, it is still a hard concept to grasp. So I usually take it a step further:

"Let me explain it another way. Let's say that I have died and I have gone before the Lord to be judged. Satan is the prosecuting attorney. As I stand before God, Satan says, 'Nancy Golden did this, and this and this.' The list goes on and on ... and there is nothing I can say to deny it—I did do all of those sinful things that Satan has listed. As I stand condemned in the guilt of my sin and God raises His gavel to pronounce His verdict that would send me to hell for eternity, Jesus steps forward and quietly says, 'Father, wait. This one is mine. I have already paid the fine.' Because Jesus has made me righteous through the blood He shed on the cross in my place, I am able to enter heaven.[35] Romans 8:1 says, 'Therefore, there is now no condemnation for those who are in Christ Jesus.'"

There are many ways to explain the Gospel and as long as they stay true to Scripture, you can use any of them that you are comfortable with and feel led to use.

Five Steps

Remember our evangelism tool box? We talked a little about *Share Jesus Without Fear* when we were discussing the Direct

Single Encounter Approach. Bill Fay outlines five steps for knowing Jesus Christ:[36]

1. Admit to God you are a sinner.
2. Wanting forgiveness for your sin.
3. Believe in your heart that Jesus Christ died on the cross for you and rose again.
4. Be willing to surrender your life to Jesus Christ.
5. Receive Jesus Christ as your Lord and Savior.

Fay goes on to explain that to receive Jesus, you can pray what is commonly known as the Sinner's Prayer.

I am actually a big fan of Fay's steps and methods *when combined with the relational approach*. After trust has been built, Fay's method can be very effective in helping a person make a commitment—*when they are ready*. And if they are not ready, you have just watered the garden so that it can continue to grow more receptive to the Holy Spirit working in their heart.

If a person decides to commit their life to Christ, you can pray with them. It doesn't have to follow these exact words, but it gives you some guidelines as to the important elements.

What is most important is not the words, but the work going on in the person's heart. How he or she articulates their need for Jesus can be very individual. Some people are very expressive, while others are very introspective.

There is no right or wrong way. We are not looking for a polished performance, what really counts is the state of a person's heart and their true desire to turn to God in repentance for their sins, recognizing that it is through the death of Jesus on the cross and His resurrection that brings reconciliation and eternal life to those who believe in Him and surrender their lives to Him.

The Sinner's Prayer

"Heavenly Father, I am a sinner. I want forgiveness for all of my sins. Father, I believe in my heart that Jesus Christ died on the cross for me and rose again. I give you my life to do with as you wish. *If I have been walking astray from your Word and will, I come back to begin again.* Father, I want Jesus to come into my life. Fill me with you, Father. Come into my life, come into my heart, Lord Jesus. I love you. I ask this in Christ's name. Amen."[37]

A Word About Prodigals

Notice the sentence I italicized in the prayer. I would like to say a word about prodigals. God has a special place in His heart for His children that have wandered away. He tells us all about it in the parable of the prodigal son in Luke 15:11-32. God loves us so much that when we turn away from Him, He is heartbroken, waiting hopefully for our return. When we do—He runs to meet us!

If you know someone who has fallen away, perhaps you can lovingly remind them that God is waiting for them to come home with His arms open wide ... and keep them in prayer for them to come home again.

For Those Who Are Uncertain of Their Salvation

Dave Earley in his book *Evangelism Is ...* asks if you are absolutely certain that you are born again. He suggests that if you have any doubt, you can respond to God today and receive His assurance.[38] I personally pray the Sinner's Prayer every time it is offered, as a way to search myself and renew my commitment to my Lord and Savior.

If you are like me, you may have had one or several occasions where you have doubted your own eternal security. Am I really saved? Having struggled with this issue myself, I know how difficult it can be. I hope I can put your fears to rest as mine now are, or if you have never experienced doubt, perhaps you will be able to help a friend who has, by reading "I Hope I'm Good Enough" in Appendix F.

QUESTIONS FOR DISCUSSION

1. What are the essential elements when presenting the Gospel story?
2. What are some of the different ways you can present the Gospel? Which way are you most comfortable with?
3. What should you do if your friend becomes uncomfortable or reluctant?
4. How do you think you should pray with your friend if they indicate that they want to receive Christ as their Lord and Savior?
5. Have you ever struggled with being unsure that you are truly saved? If so, can you identify why? You may have, like the lady in Tractor Supply, wondered if you were good enough. After reading Appendix F, what steps can you take right now, so that you can be completely confident in your salvation?

7

BUT WHAT ABOUT THE BUDDHISTS?

Considering Folks Who Follow a Different Religion

What do we do about all of the people we meet who already follow a religion and probably grew up with the beliefs they have? Buddhists, Muslims, Hindus, and many other adherents of non-Christian faiths are often devout in their religious beliefs and practice. With our global economy, more and more of these folks are in our neighborhoods and work-places. How do we approach these people with the Gospel?

My husband Phil works for a company that does a lot of business with China. Upper management has identified our family as their go-to resource for entertaining visitors that come from overseas, since we have a heart for people from around the world. We are very comfortable showing folks around and spending time with them, even if there is a language barrier. We often invite them to spend time with our family which they usually appreciate, since they are frequently away from their own families for long periods of time, traveling on business.

On this particular occasion, we were going out to dinner at a local restaurant with a sales representative from Hong Kong who works for one of the companies that Phil's employer does business with. This man is Asian and speaks multiple languages. He was here with his boss who owns the factory in China that manufactures their products. He often serves as an interpreter for his boss, who speaks limited English. A third person, one of their engineers who does not speak any English, was also in our party that evening.

Our then twelve year old son Josh was also accompanying us to dinner that night. All of the Asian men were delighted to meet Josh and even more so when he greeted them in Chinese. The factory owner in particular was quite taken with Josh and asked him to come for a visit to China, extending an invitation for Josh to stay in his home, which is quite an honor in Chinese culture.

We sat around the table in the restaurant and chatted about their families and the places they had visited. When the food was served, we explained to our new friends that we have a family tradition—we like to hold hands and pray over our meal together. We told them that we consider them part of our family too and would they like to hold hands and pray with us?

This situation has probably occurred a hundred times and our request has always been greeted with smiles and eager participation, regardless of the religious beliefs of our guests. This evening was no exception and we got to hold hands and pray with our new friends. We always include in our prayer a desire for God to bless their families and gratitude for getting to spend time with them.

After we prayed and started eating our food, the conversation turned to matters of faith. The factory owner was very eager to share that when he was at home he went to the temple and prayed to Buddha every day. We responded by telling him how wonderful that was, and how important it is to have faith as part of our daily lives. It was very interesting to observe the expression on Josh's face during this conversation.

Eventually, the talk turned to their families and how our customs and traditions are different, but our family values are very similar. The evening ended on a pleasant note as we said goodbye, and we planned to meet again the next day for one more visit before their return to China.

On the trip home, it was obvious that Josh was about to explode with a question he had. He had sat through the evening observing his parents interacting with people from China who prayed to Buddha, and we had not once tried to tell them the error of their ways! We had not gotten very far down the road when he burst out, "Why, Mom?!! Why didn't you tell them that Jesus is the only way?!!!!"

I was so proud of Josh for keeping control of himself and not asking his question until we had parted with our guests, because it was very obvious he had been struggling with this question internally over dinner. I was also proud of his concern, that he wanted our new friends to understand that Jesus was the way, the truth and the life so that they could have eternal life, rather than worshipping a false god that could not save them.

However, this was a great opportunity for Josh to understand how to witness to others through relationship. Phil responded to Josh's question by asking him, "How would you feel if you had just met someone and they told you that you were going to hell because your religion was wrong?" I explained that their most likely response would be, that it would make them really mad – they would be thinking, "Who do those people think they are, telling me that my religion is wrong and theirs is right?"

So What Can You Do In These Types Of Situations?

1. You can wear your Christianity on your sleeve—you make it clear that you are a Christian but you do so in a non-threatening manner. Requesting to pray over a meal together is a great example of how you can make your faith public. I usually wear a cross necklace because I appreciate the reminder of my Lord's sacrifice as a great way to also share with others that I am a Christ follower.

2. The intent is to relate loving actions with being a Christ follower. By offering assistance and spending time with folks that follow a different religion, you have an opportunity to show the love of Christ in tangible ways, which serves as a very compelling witness.

3. Do not tell the person that their religion is wrong. Ask questions and find common ground (A Buddhist goes to temple, a Christian goes to church).

4. Trust in God's plan for the person you are witnessing to. If this is the only chance you will have to see him, trust in the leading of the Holy Spirit and if you never have the chance to bring up the Gospel, trust that you have planted a seed and God will bring someone else into their life to draw them to Him.

5. If you do have an opportunity to explain the Gospel, don't try to force a decision. You can invite the other person to explain their religious beliefs without either party feeling threatened. The truth will always lead to Jesus, but you must remember that the person in front of you may have spent their entire childhood and much of their adult life following their religion faithfully. It will most likely take time for them to

process the truth of the Gospel and if you are disrespectful towards their current beliefs, they will most likely close their hearts to your message.

Haircuts, Buddha, and Sharing the Gospel

PHIL AND JOSH and I all get our hair cut at the same little shop in our community. We have been going there for the past five years. Two lovely ladies from Vietnam work there and they are the ones that always cut our hair. Over the years we have formed a relationship with these two women. We have learned about their families and have shared in their accomplishments, as well as their trials.

One of these ladies received the horrifying news that she had breast cancer. We prayed for her, sent her flowers, and brought her gifts, as she went through chemotherapy. What a joy it is to see her with a full return to health!

The other lady has a son in junior high and we often talk about how he is doing in school. She loves to speak English and she always wants to improve her conversation skills. When her relatives came to the United States recently and they needed to know where they could learn English, I found local classes for them to attend.

Every Christmas we drop by the shop with Christmas presents for both of these ladies, wishing them "Merry Christmas" in Vietnamese. They know we are Christians, although we have never gotten into a truly spiritual discussion—until the other day.

The day was Phil's birthday, and we had decided to go by their shop so he could get a haircut. Usually the shop is very busy with other customers waiting in line, but on this day, that was not the case. The lady that usually cuts Phil's hair came out and got started. The other lady, who usually cuts my hair, also came out. I was not due for a hair cut yet, so we chatted a bit. I had a book with me that I was going to study, but when I saw that she was free, I invited my friend to sit down and wait with me so she could practice her English.

We began to talk about our brothers and sisters and then suddenly she asked me about God—if I can feel His presence when I pray. I said that yes, that I can and that the feeling is very wonderful and comforting. She said that she does too and she wanted to tell me about an experience that she had this past week.

She had felt very weak—she was unable to move and she didn't want to get out of bed. She had no energy at all, so she called out to Buddha and "they" came. She said that whenever she has a problem, she calls out to Buddha and "they" always come to help her. She explained that she picked up her holy book for her religion and read it for thirty minutes and then she felt much better—she was healed.

My friend was very excited to talk to me about how important it was for us to depend on our faith every day—and that Buddha comes to help her just like God comes to help me. The temptation of pluralism (believing that other religions are also paths to God) exists here, since she obviously feels very deeply that her god actively brings her comfort and also because we don't want to contemplate the fate of those who don't know Jesus as their Lord.

But God calls us to be a witness for the true living God and her eternal destiny is at stake, so we can't just go along with her story, yet we need to be sensitive and not openly rebuke it. I felt very uncomfortable because of her obvious passion for Buddha. I really wanted to show her the truth of the Gospel so she could know Jesus as her Savior, but I realized I needed to do it in such a way that did not cause her to reject what I was saying.

I agreed with my friend that it is so important to depend on

God to help us and how wonderful it is that He does. During our conversation it was easy to see that she equated my God with Buddha as both being Supreme Beings that we could turn to.

As you can imagine, this is a difficult conversation for a Christ follower to be a part of, because our first instinct is to say, "Noooooooooooo...Buddha is all wrong!" *But that is where you have to trust in and be sensitive to the leading of the Holy Spirit.*

I asked my friend if she had something to write on, and she got a blank receipt off of the pad she used for writing receipts for customers. I thanked her for it and told her that I just wanted to show her how Christianity works.

I started making my stick figures (see Gospel Illustration on a Napkin in Chapter Six). My friend started laughing when I made my hair curly and she joined in, saying to make hers straight and longer and we also needed to add in Phil and the other lady into the picture, which I did.

I explained to my friend about the role of Jesus and it was obvious that while she was listening, she wasn't grasping the concept of Jesus cleansing us of our sins and becoming our righteousness for us since we could *never* be good enough, and that it is only through Him we are able to go to heaven.

Since I wasn't having much success with my explanation, I felt led to ask her to explain how her religion works. She took the receipt from me and drew three parallel lines:

_____

_____

_____

She told me that every line was a level, and that each level represented a type of existence. If a person was on the bottom line, life would be very difficult, with lots of problems. Someone on the middle line was experiencing a life that wasn't as hard as the bottom level, but still had challenges and problems. The top level was the best level—life was good with a wonderful family and not any difficult problems. Every person lived many lives and it was the person's job to do good things in order to move to the upper level.

She drew a circular arrow around all three lines that showed the levels were a cycle – you could repeat the same level many times, drop down to the lower level, or move up to the upper level and drop down to a lower level – it all depended on how much good or bad you did in each life as to where you would land next. She wrote the word "heaven" above the parallel lines. Eventually, you would do enough good to be able to go to heaven, but it could take many lifetimes to get there; she drew an arrow from the top level towards heaven.

Her picture resided next to my Gospel illustration on the same piece of paper. I took the piece of paper and pointed at the levels and asked, "So you have to keep trying over and over again to be good enough to go to heaven and you don't know how many lifetimes that will be or when you are good enough?" and my friend said that I was correct. So I pointed from the cross to heaven and said, "In the Christian religion, we go directly to heaven."

My friend took her finger and also pointed at heaven. With some amazement in her voice she asked, "You get to go directly to heaven?" I said, "Yes, we know that we can never be good enough, so it is only through Jesus that we can get to heaven. If we ask Him into our heart and commit our life to Him, we go directly to heaven."

The Differences are Profound!

Pastor Chad Burton points out what we should do when witnessing to those of other faiths; rather than arrogantly approaching them with a "my faith is better than yours" atti-tude, he says, "We emphasize the uniqueness of Jesus compared to these other leaders. Jesus alone claims to be God incarnate, dies an atoning death for the sins of humanity, rises from the dead, sits at the right hand of God and will one day judge the quick and the dead."

Other religions are works-based and the freedom that can be found in Christ is very attractive once it is explained. But we are not "marketing" Jesus even though His superiority becomes obvious when compared with other religions. Ultimately, we are sharing our faith in order for the Holy Spirit to do a work in a person's heart that draws them to the very truth of the Gospel message.

I know my friend was intrigued by the thought of a direct route to heaven and that may cause her to have a desire to learn more. So what is my job? To continue to get my hair cuts with her and continue to love her like I have been doing for the past five years. I especially need to be sensitive to the leading of the Holy Spirit as I interact with her in the future.

As we got up to leave, I joked and asked if she would like to keep my "art work," and she smiled and said yes. I handed her the receipt with our drawings on it; perhaps she will look at that receipt in the future and feel a stirring in her heart when she sees the cross forming a bridge directly to God.

For additional help in improving your communication skills, please read over Appendix G.

QUESTIONS FOR DISCUSSION

1. Have you ever been in a situation where you wanted to share your faith with someone of a different faith? If yes, how did you proceed and how did they respond?

2. When you see a non-Christian talk about their religion with passionate belief, how does that make

you feel? How are some ways you can respond in obedience to the Great Commission without offending them?

3. Are there specific areas in Appendix G that you need to work on? Keep this list available and review it every few weeks, so that you can see where you are improving and what areas you need to continue to work on.

4. Do you have to present the Gospel in every encounter you have with someone of a different faith? Why or why not?

5. You have made friends with someone of a different faith, but they don't show much interest in talking about spiritual things. How should you proceed?

6. Your Hindu friend views Jesus as one of many paths that all lead to heaven. How can you explain the difference between Jesus and all of the religious leaders in history?

7. HOMEWORK: If you are reading this as part of an evangelism class, be prepared to share the Gospel with a partner for next week's class. You can do this according to your own personal strategy using any of the concepts that you have learned, one of your own that we have not gone over, or any combination that you feel would be effective in your own evangelism endeavors. If you are not part of a class, prepare your personal evangelism strategy and plan on finding a friend that you can practice with.

8

WITNESSING IN THE WORKPLACE

Is It Possible to be a Christian Witness in the Workplace?

Many people would like to share about their faith in the workplace but are hesitant, and understandably so. Their very jobs may depend on how they present themselves to others. So, how does someone go about sharing the Gospel at work? It all goes back to what we have been learning about – building relationships of trust and following as the Holy Spirit leads.

How Would I Go About It Without Coming Off as Trying to Push My Beliefs on Others?

As a follower of Christ, you have a unique opportunity from day one. Because your identity is in Christ, you just need to be yourself. That might not mean bringing a Bible into work meetings, but it certainly means reflecting Christ's love in your daily interactions. Be an encourager to those around you. Only engage in wholesome talk – resist participating in office gossip.
1 Peter 2:9,

But you are a chosen people, a royal priesthood, a holy nation,
God's special possession, that you may declare the praises of
him who called you out of darkness into his wonderful light.

As a Christ-follower, you represent Jesus in the workplace.
You can build a reputation as someone who is sincerely interested in the well-being of others. You can offer help when you
see an opportunity to serve others. You can start meetings with a
cordial greeting and ask others about aspects of their lives you
have heard them talk about. If your co-worker's son has an
upcoming hockey game later that day, inquire the next day
about how it went. As time goes on, you will be viewed as
someone who cares about those around you.

When difficulties arrive at work, adopt an attitude of help-
fulness and encouragement. Avoid pointing fingers or assigning
blame, but rather, focus on positive ways to come up with a solu-
tion that helps everyone. Affirm your co-workers privately and
publicly. If you have a problem with someone, practice the
biblical principles found in Matthew 18:15-17 and try to resolve
the issue you have with that person between you and them first,
before escalating it.

You can also sprinkle in your faith naturally when talking to
your co-workers. How wonderful it is to show them God's provi-
sion in your life! If you are in a very stressful situation, you can
be a witness to the peace you have in Christ as you walk through
it. You can also let your co-workers know you are praying for
them if they share about a difficult situation in their lives.

What Might That Look Like?

Just as I have emphasized in previous chapters, the Holy
Spirit is active, and He will provide opportunities for you. Your
job is to be alert for those opportunities. One example I can

think of is the relationship I developed with a senior manager during the pandemic.

We were all working remotely. English was not his first language, and he was often required to write papers that would be utilized by upper management. I offered to provide editing for him as the need arose. Over the next few months, I would occasionally have an email from him waiting in my inbox, with a Word file he requested I edit. I was glad to do so and provided him with a quick turnaround. While outside of the scope of my responsibilities, it was a very tangible way I could show Christ to this person.

Over time, we developed a friendship and started sharing about our families. His wife and children were here, but the rest of his family was in India. It was a dreadful time because the deadly COVID-19 Delta variant was surging in India.

One day, he reached out to let me know his father had Covid and was in the hospital. The medical workers there were very overextended, and he was leaving the next day to fly to India to be with his father and advocate for him. Not knowing his religious affiliation, I asked if I could pray for him. He immediately nodded and bowed his head.

I had the honor of praying for my co-worker and his family over that remote call. I couldn't resist opening my eyes as I prayed to see if he was okay with it. My heart leapt in my chest as I could see his eyes tightly shut and his face in a pose of intense concentration. What a privilege to be able to pray for this man I had never met in person but had developed a friendship with at work!

During that time, it was very difficult to obtain any N95 masks. An N95 mask offers the best protection from being infected and is superior to other types of masks. My co-worker would be on an airplane at increased risk of exposure in close quarters with other passengers for around 15 hours. Upon his arrival, he would be at the hospital, where the horrific Delta variant was rampant.

I had a pack of a dozen N95s that I had in case of emergency. I called my co-worker to find out if he had any N95s, and he said no, he didn't. I found out he lived about 45 minutes from us and asked for his address. I messaged my manager that I had an important errand to run and grabbed the package of N95s. My husband Phil and I jumped in the car and headed to his house.

Upon our arrival, I noticed a statue of Buddha on my co-worker's porch – giving me an obvious clue as to his religion. We left the N95s in a bag in front of his door, because COVID-19 was raging here as well, making visiting impossible. I called my co-worker from my cell phone to let him know that the N95s were on his porch. We stood by our car, smiling and waving, as we watched him come out the front door and get the bag. He smiled and waved back, and we left feeling very grateful that God had used us to help provide for his journey.

Fast-forward to a few days later. My co-worker had been messaging me occasionally about his father's condition, which, in the beginning, was very scary due to the severity of his illness —when I received a video call on our Teams channel at work. My co-worker was at the other end of the call, in a dimly lit bedroom. There is about a twelve-hour difference between where I live and India – so it was about 2:00 am there.

He looked exhausted, but his smile told the story before he started speaking. He was calling to let me know that his father had turned the corner, the treatment he had been receiving was working, and he was going to be okay. Hallelujah!

I am still astonished and humbled when I think about my co-worker calling me at 2:00 am his time to share the happy news.

What an amazing privilege it is when God calls us to minister to someone as His ambassador! When my co-worker eventually returned to his home in the United States, we continued our friendship, and the Holy Spirit provided further opportunities for spiritual conversations.

My co-worker appreciated it when I prayed during those conversations and he shared that he had visited Christian churches in the past. I believe the Holy Spirit is drawing my co-worker to Jesus, and I am so blessed that He used me as part of that work.

As I write this, it has been over a year since my co-worker left to work for another company, which requires frequent traveling and exhausting days for him. However, we are still connected on social media and keep in touch.

Perhaps the Holy Spirit will provide additional opportunities for the seeds He planted through me to be watered, or maybe He will use someone else. Regardless, the results are His. The Holy Spirit's divine intervention can touch a person's heart, leading them into a saving relationship with our Lord and Savior. Praise God!

Can you see how the trust I had built enabled me to minister to my co-worker in a very unexpected way? God is like that, I think. He will use us in ways we would scarcely imagine for ourselves, and He will provide us with the ability and means to do it.

I think that sometimes we need to choose the hard thing because it enables us to be an effective minister. I had to cross cultural, religious, and social boundaries (I am not in senior management) to form a friendship with my co-worker. The Holy Spirit provided ways for me to offer tangible help (editing papers, N95s), which evolved into intangible service (supportive presence, prayer).

This didn't happen overnight, and in some cases, it challenged me and got me out of my comfort zone. I want to encourage you to be open to the opportunities the Holy Spirit brings to you, and not be afraid to be stretched. Great things can happen if you are willing to choose the hard thing.

You are an Ambassador for Christ Wherever You Are!

While my previous example is a bit dramatic, your ministry at work can consist of simply being a caring presence. Being a good listener and providing a safe space for your co-workers can go a long way in developing trust which will enable the Holy Spirit to open opportunities for you to minister.

You may work with people from different faiths or people with a very secular faith or no faith at all. Remember that no one wants to be told that their way of thinking is wrong, so you will need to tread carefully. This does not mean you don't have conviction, but it does mean that you want your audience to receive what you feel led to say – and so it is very important to be respectful. 1 Peter 3:15-16 tells us:

> But in your hearts revere Christ as Lord. Always be prepared to give an answer to everyone who asks you to give the reason for the hope that you have. But do this with gentleness and respect, keeping a clear conscience, so that those who speak maliciously against your good behavior in Christ may be ashamed of their slander.

So, how can you go about this, and when should you? When your heart aches for those who don't know Christ, how can you tell them about Him in a loving way so that they will receive your words? The Holy Spirit will guide you in that.

Make sure you approach the task prayerfully and be discerning – tailor what you say to how the person is responding. Sometimes, you will sense you should stop; other times, you will know to continue past what you ever dreamed possible. Lean into the Holy Spirit and His guidance.

My heart was troubled because I so much wanted to share about Jesus, but I also didn't want people to reject hearing about Him because they thought I was being pushy. I wrote the blog post you will find in Appendix H in response to that. I have shared it on social media, and I have sent the link to people that God put on my heart. While you won't be able to see the video unless you go to my blog – you'll get the general idea and you can also find the web address to my blog at the end of the appendix.

Pray for how God is leading you in the mission field of your workplace. Be attentive to the leading of the Holy Spirit. He may guide you in ways that surprise you! Be salt and light – to God's glory and for the salvation of your co-workers!

QUESTIONS FOR DISCUSSION

1. Does it make you nervous to think about sharing your faith at work? If so, what makes you feel that way?

2. How can you live out your identity in Christ at work?

3. One of your co-workers seems troubled. What might you do to show you care and are available to talk if they desire?

4. What are some tangible ways you can show the love of Christ to an individual at work? To a group?

5. What are some intangible ways you can show the love of Christ to an individual at work? To a group?

6. A co-worker is obviously enmeshed in new-age spirituality. How should you conduct your interactions with them?

7. What boundaries would you have to cross in your own workplace in order to be an ambassador for Christ? Does that look impossible? Can you seek guidance from God and allow His Holy Spirit to lead you in that effort?

8. Do you feel the same quandary I sometimes feel? Now that I have established a relationship of trust, how do I move that into a spiritual discussion where I can share about Jesus? You can write a blog post (or use mine), but ultimately, the answer is always going to be the same. What do you think the answer is? HINT: It is a founding principle that has been exhorted throughout this book.

9

WHAT HAPPENS NEXT?

Essential Elements For A True Conversion

While this topic is seldom talked about, it is an important one. Some well-meaning Christians in their enthusiasm to bring others to Christ may depend solely on a person's verbal affirmation. But what does it really mean to become a committed disciple of the Lord Jesus Christ?

Earley addresses this important issue in his book and writes that there are two sides to conversion, a turning towards God (faith) and a turning away from sin (repentance).[39] He goes further and explains that conversion is felt on three levels: intellect, emotion, and will.

In order to truly be converted, a person must know the basic elements of the Gospel: the death, burial and resurrection of Jesus for our sins. They must feel the guilt and shame of their sins and be drawn to Christ as Savior. They must also act upon their knowledge and feelings with a changed life, turning from sin and relying on Christ alone for salvation. A true conversion not only penetrates a person's intellect and emotions, it affects their will as well, resulting in a change of behavior.[40]

Earley offers another version of the Sinner's Prayer, in which he expands on the basic truths that are presented in Fay's version and incorporates the elements of true conversion: knowing, feeling, AND acting:

Dear God,

I admit that I have sinned. I admit that my religion alone is not going to give me a relationship with You. I admit that my goodness is not good enough. I admit that I need to be born again.

I believe that Jesus is God's Son. I believe that Jesus never sinned. I believe that Jesus died to pay for my sins. I believe that Jesus rose from the dead to give me eternal life.

Right now I call upon the Name of the Lord Jesus to save me. I ask the Holy Spirit to come into my heart and make me a new person. I ask that I may be born again as a child of God. I surrender the throne of my heart to you. I ask to experience Your love and power.

I am willing to do anything You tell me to do. I am willing to stop doing anything that displeases You. I ask for the power to follow You all the days of my life.

In Jesus' name. Amen.[41]

A person first coming to faith in Jesus is a baby in their knowledge of Him and at the very beginning of their spiritual journey. What is most important is the condition of the person's heart. Their understanding and response to God's gift of unconditional love and forgiveness, their willingness to repent from their sins, and that they have a *true desire* to commit their life to Jesus Christ as their Lord and Savior, are all essential elements that reflect a true conversion.

One thing I love about this prayer is that we are leaning into God for His help in following Him. Notice the final sentence, "I ask for the power to follow You all the days of my life." We are not in it alone. God is right there with us and when we find ourselves faltering, He will strengthen us. Praise God!

A Word About Spiritual Birthdays

While some people place an emphasis on Spiritual Birthdays, which are usually defined as the exact moment that a person recalls their decision to come to Christ—not every Christian has one. This speaks to the process of conversion. When someone receives Jesus Christ as their Lord and Savior, they are born again and receive the Holy Spirit to dwell in them.

But I am an example of someone not knowing the moment of my own conversion. I can't recall when I actually accepted my faith as my own. I just know that I have, and I am okay with that. The main idea is that there is evidence in the person's life as to whether their conversion is real or not. Jesus explains in Matthew 7:16-23,

> By their fruit you will recognize them. Do people pick grapes from thornbushes, or figs from thistles? Likewise every good tree bears good fruit, but a bad tree bears bad fruit. A good tree cannot bear bad fruit, and a bad tree cannot bear good fruit. Every tree that does not bear good fruit is cut down and thrown into the fire. Thus, by their fruit you will recognize them.

In John 13:34-35 Jesus teaches us,

> A new command I give you: Love one another. As I have loved you, so you must love one another. By this all men will know that you are my disciples, if you love one another.

Sanctification, the Role of the Holy Spirit in the Life of the Believer, and Discipleship

Although these topics are beyond the scope of our book, they are important enough to mention. Once a person has accepted Jesus Christ as Lord and Savior – their journey is just beginning! They are like newborns in their faith and just like newborns, they need to be nurtured. What you do next can have a huge impact on their spiritual journey.

Notice that in Matthew 28:19-20, Jesus commands us to *make disciples*. We have a responsibility to help our friend grow in his or her relationship with Christ. While a lot of their questions may have been answered during the time they were seeking Christ, topics like the in-dwelling of the Holy Spirit and sanctification are probably better understood when one is experiencing it for themselves, rather than simply as an abstract theory.

The great thing about relational evangelism is that you have already established a relationship with that person. It's simply a matter of including them in your spiritual activities, inviting them to go to church with you, and introducing them to other Christians. Perhaps there is a Bible study or class you can accompany them to. Celebrate their new found identity in Christ with them and invite others to do so as well!

Discipleship and Community in the Body of Christ

God calls us to live in community with one another in the Body of Christ and to minister to one another as a royal priesthood of believers (1 Peter 2:9). If someone comes to Christ but is left on their own afterwards, at best they won't know how to grow in their faith and at worst they will be tempted to fall into their old sinful habits.

In Chapter 7 of the Book of Romans, we learn about the

constant struggle between the flesh and the spirit, and Paul writes in verses 18-19,

> I know that nothing good lives in me, that is, in my sinful nature. For I have the desire to do what is good, but I cannot carry it out. For what I do is not the good I want to do; no, the evil I do not want to do—this I keep on doing.

If even the Apostle Paul struggled with sin, it seems safe to say that it is a part of the human condition even after conversion. By teaching a new believer to practice spiritual disciplines (such as praying and reading the Bible) and providing a mentoring relationship, they can mature in their faith and build on their foundation of trusting in Christ.

Scripture clearly shows us that the Christian journey was not meant to be travelled alone and for good reason—while we always need to be dependent on the Holy Spirit, sometimes we need fellow believers to help us along, no matter what stage we are at on our journey. Hebrews 10:25 tells us,

> Let us not give up meeting together, as some are in the habit of doing, but let us encourage one another—and all the more as you see the Day approaching.

Programs that are already in place can reach out to people and create opportunities for discipleship that benefit everyone. Multiple opportunities that fit different people and different levels of maturity provide fellowship, spiritual growth, and opportunities to serve. Small groups, classes, informal gatherings, and a mentoring program are some of the ways we can meet the need for community and discipleship.

Not everyone is comfortable or has time for small groups. Some folks prefer attending a class and some would appreciate having a mentor available to them who could disciple them over a cup of coffee. Some people are very self-motivated and others need encouragement to participate. By providing a variety of opportunities, different needs can be met to facilitate the spiritual growth of not only new believers, but all of the members of the church body.

A READING LIST has been added in Appendix H which includes some books on evangelism that can help answer any questions that you may have and are good additions to anyone's spiritual library.

QUESTIONS FOR DISCUSSION

1. What are the elements for a true conversion? What are some indications noted in Scripture that suggest a person has truly turned their life over to Christ?
2. If a person within your sphere of influence is representing themselves as a Christian but their behavior indicates otherwise, how should you respond and why?
3. What can you do to nurture a new believer?
4. What are some ways your church can provide discipleship for a new believer?
5. Select one of the books from Appendix H that catches your interest and make it a point to get a copy for further study.
6. If you are in an evangelism class, take turns with others in your class on presenting the Gospel in your own personal style. Present the Gospel to at least three other class members. If you are not a part of a class, make sure and practice with a friend.

7. Make a commitment to your own personalized plan of evangelism. Make it real—write it down and make plans with your classmates or friends to get together periodically to encourage and support each other, to share stories of how God is working in your lives and to celebrate even baby steps in your efforts to be obedient to the Great Commission.

I LOVE TO TELL THE STORY

1 I love to tell the story
of unseen things above,
of Jesus and his glory,
of Jesus and his love.
I love to tell the story
because I know it's true;
it satisfies my longings
as nothing else can do.
Refrain:
I love to tell the story;
'twill be my theme in glory
to tell the old, old story
of Jesus and his love.
2 [A seasonal stanza may be sung.]
3 I love to tell the story,
for those who know it best
seem hungering and thirsting
to hear it like the rest.
And when in scenes of glory
I sing the new, new song,

'twill be the old, old story
that I have loved so long.
[Christ's Birth]
4 An angel brought glad tidings:
"Send all your fears away,
for Christ, your Lord and Savior,
is born for you this day."
Then many other angels
sang praise for Jesus' birth:
"To God on high be glory,
and peace to all the earth." [Refrain]
5 [Christ's Death]
Christ Jesus, pure and holy,
without a spot or stain,
by wicked hands was taken,
was crucified and slain!
And now the word is finished,
the sinner's debt is paid,
because on Christ the Righteous
the sin of all was laid. [Refrain]
[Christ's Resurrection]
6 O wonderful redemption!
The price for sin is paid,
salvation is accomplished,
my heart is unafraid,
for God has raised Christ Jesus
to show the work was done;
his glorious resurrection
declared the vict'ry won! [Refrain]
[Christ's Commission]
7 The Savior of all people
has brought his peace to you;
now go and tell the story,

for others need it too.
To ev'ry land and nation
ring out the gospel call;
proclaim that Christ is risen
and grants his peace to all. [Refrain]

I love to tell the story Of unseen things above
    Author: A. Kate Hankey (1866); Author (refrain): William G. Fischer (1869)

Psalm 66:16,

    Come and hear, all you who fear God;
      let me tell you what he has done for me.

    Thank you for your heart for the Great Commission!

CONGRATULATIONS!

You have completed what I pray has been a journey that has helped you to feel confident in carrying out your desire to share your faith—in obedience to the One who gave everything for us. Jesus was the ultimate missionary—He left the glories of heaven to come to the earth as His mission field—surely we can bring the Gospel to those in our Jerusalem!

In our obedience to the Great Commission and the Second Greatest Commandment, we can look forward to that great day in Matthew 25:21, "His master replied, 'Well done, good and faithful servant! You have been faithful with a few things; I will put you in charge of many things. Come and share your master's happiness!'"

May God bless you and your efforts to share the Gospel as you join Him on mission!

APPENDIX A

A JEWISH CONTEXTUALIZATION OF THE GOSPEL

We decided to have our Thanksgiving dinner on Friday instead of Thursday so that all of our family members could be present. My eighty-seven-year-old mother is Jewish, and although through the years I have spoken with her about Jesus on many occasions, she always had some hesitation. She would say that Jesus is the Savior, but I always felt she did so just to please me and that she never really grasped who He really is.

A book critique on *The Four Views on Hell* that I had been working on all week for my theology class had brought the issue of eternal life for my mom, always lingering in the background of my mind, to the forefront. We decided to have communion as part of our Thanksgiving celebration and her hesitation was extremely evident, which seemed to confirm my reason for concern.

I felt an urge to talk to her which I believe was the Holy Spirit prompting me. The thought had crossed my mind earlier but I had dismissed it, thinking it would not be a good time after all of the chaos of grandkids running through the house. But the Holy Spirit knew better! So after the kids left to go to the movies,

I asked my mom if I could talk to her about what I was learning at school.

When we first began our discussion, Mom mentioned that we were still waiting for the Messiah. She had never made the connection of Jesus as Savior being Jesus as Messiah, and I had the wonderful privilege of explaining to her that Jesus the Savior is Jesus the Messiah.

I came to find out that one of her obstacles to fully committing to Jesus was the prejudice she experienced in growing up when people found out she was Jewish. I explained to her that was the evil of men and did not have anything to do with Jesus or true Christianity. Unfortunately, we are all sinners and often hurt each other.

I was then able to paint for her a beautiful picture of Israel's role in God's redemptive plan and the critical role that Israel had as God's instrument to save humanity. I talked to her about the Abrahamic covenant and about the Davidic covenant and all of God's promises in the Old Testament culminating in Jesus as Messiah.

Being able to present it from a Jewish standpoint made it understandable for her. It was through my study of *Knowing Jesus Through the Old Testament* (one of the books assigned for a seminary class I was currently taking) that I was able to accomplish this—I pulled it out and read her some key passages, along with Scripture. Using some of the methods I had learned in my evangelism class gave me structure as we talked and our conversation culminated in Mom committing her life to Jesus and praying the Sinner's Prayer together!

My mom said that our conversation enabled her to overcome the obstacles that had been keeping her from fully committing to Christ, Praise God!!! I believe that God brought me to Liberty Baptist Theological Seminary and to be in those particular classes for "such a time as this," and I thank God that I could be an instrument for the Holy Spirit to use in opening my mother's heart to the love of Jesus, so that she could enter into her own personal relationship with Jesus the Messiah.

APPENDIX B

THAT'S NOT A PROSTITUTE

In Chapter 5 of Duane Elmer's book, *Cross-Cultural Servanthood*, he deals with acceptance and how to communicate respect to others. Simply put, it is the ability to "communicate value, worth and esteem to another person," and Elmer grounds his discussion in Romans 15:7, "Accept one another, then, just as Christ accepted you, in order to bring praise to God." One of the highlights of this chapter is Elmer's exploration of dignity. The story he tells of "That's not a Prostitute" had a profound effect on me.

He writes of the time he was out on the streets with his friend, Mark Van Houten, in order to minister to people. He was walking with Mark, who was familiar with the territory and experienced in street ministry, when Elmer saw a scantily clad woman on a street corner. He lowered his voice so as not to be heard by the woman and asked Mark, "Is she a prostitute?" Mark paused and then replied firmly, "No! That's not a prostitute. That's a *person* ... in prostitution."

Mark's statement clarified my view of a friend of mine for me, not as a crack cocaine addict, but rather, as a man (precious child of God made in His image) with a crack cocaine addiction. We received the devastating news that he died (he was only fifty-years-old), but we are also rejoicing because it was through his most difficult times that two men from church stepped forward to minister and witness to him and he accepted Jesus as His Lord and Savior.

They cared enough to see him first and foremost as "a human being loved by God, accepted by Christ, sacredly endowed with dignity and worthy of being treated with respect and honor by every other human being." He is more than a conqueror in heaven with Jesus now, and it is through the lens of Jesus that I think of him. Elmer's powerful words serve as affirmation: his addiction did not define him; his identity is and always will be in Christ.

APPENDIX C

THE MISSION FIELD IN OUR OWN BACKYARD

Are you thinking about taking a mission trip but not sure about traveling to a foreign country? In Acts 1:8, Jesus tells his disciples, "But you will receive power when the Holy Spirit comes on you; and you will be my witnesses in Jerusalem, and in all Judea and Samaria, and to the ends of the earth." After His words, Jesus ascends into heaven, leaving His disciples with a mission, the same one we share today: through the power of the Holy Spirit we are to bring the gospel to a world that desperately needs a Savior.

So where do you fit in the big picture? Not everyone is called to witness in the same places. And the truth of the matter is, much of our international mission field does not even require a plane ticket; they have come to us and live in our own neighborhood.

The intent is not to discourage those of us who are led to travel the globe in order to spread the Good News, but to remind those of us who are not able to travel that opportunities still abound in our own backyard. The immigrant population of our country has exploded in recent years and most cities boast areas with ethnic concentrations from other countries.

Try to imagine what it must be like to be an immigrant in the United States today. Often people arrive here from great personal sacrifice. They may come from difficult situations in their native countries ranging from persecution to struggling to meet the basic needs of their families and dreaming for something more. A common thread of desire is found in each individual that enters our country—the desire for better opportunities for themselves and especially for their children.

Imagine being in a country where you do not understand the language. This isn't a vacation destination; this place is to be your home. But you can't communicate. You want to participate in your children's education and take part in your community, but you are limited by the language barrier.

Many of these folks that live among us feel isolated and lonely. And they are everywhere. They are your neighbors down the street. They live in the apartment complex by the grocery store where you shop. Their children attend the same schools as your children.

As an ESL (English as a Second Language) teacher for an adult education center in a North Texas community, and as a volunteer in ESL ministries at local churches, I have been able to experience first-hand the dreams of many of the immigrants in our area. Each new class brings a roomful of hard working students, many of whom are morning students starting their day with English class before going to their jobs or they are evening students and have already completed a full day's work.

Teaching at the beginning level, God has provided me with a wonderful opportunity to minister to these folks. Most of my students are very nervous on the first day of class. They have not been to school in years and are now finding themselves in an English class with no idea of what to expect. My first task is not to teach English, but to help the students feel comfortable, happy, and excited to be there.

Our classroom must feel like a safe and welcoming place before learning can occur. In the process we all get to know each other and as the semester progresses, we become a family. Amazing things happen. Students learn of the love of Jesus as their needs are met and they in turn volunteer to help others. Lifelong friendships form and real learning takes place.

Let me tell you about Juan, one of my younger students. We had been studying emotions that week. Classes were Monday through Thursday, so on Thursday I gave my students some homework to do over the weekend.

I ended the class with my usual admonition to my students to practice their English. Their assignment for this particular weekend was to write three sentences based on what we had learned about feelings and emotions. For example, "I am happy because my mother is here for a visit." "I am tired because I worked overtime this week."

When my students returned on Monday, I did my usual routine of greeting students individually at their desks, and asked them to show me their homework. This routine guaranteed that I gave each student some personal attention and provided an opportunity to find out if there were any concerns that the student might be having.

That particular day I had gone down each row of my class and I had gotten an interesting variety of answers to the homework assignment. "I am excited because my son's soccer team won Saturday." "I am lonely because I miss my family." "I am sad because my father died in a car accident this weekend."

I stopped in shock. "What ... Juan, is this true? Did this happen?" I desperately hoped that this was a simple matter of miscommunication which happened very frequently with my students. I did not speak Juan's native language so I was depending on him to be able to communicate with me in English.

My usually tough and always joking and smiling eighteen-year-old student looked at me with tears in his eyes. "Yes, Teacher," he said. "It's true." My heart dropped in my chest. "Oh, Juan, I am so sorry." I hugged him and started praying as he cried in my arms.

The rest of the class was a blur as I sought to find help for Juan. The reality of his situation was that he was living with his two older brothers and worked in a restaurant busing tables, and had no means to return to his native country for the funeral. It was understood by his family that he would remain here, immersed in his grief and unable to seek the comfort of the home he grew up in or that of his family members still living there.

My husband and I did our best to love and comfort Juan, but we felt so helpless; we wished we could do more. Juan bore his grief and continued his classes and work. But the light was gone from his eyes.

That was over three years ago, and I still get a phone call from Juan occasionally. What a blessing it was to hear the smile back in his voice the last time we talked. While it has probably been over a year now since our last conversation (he has moved to a different state), I know he carries in his heart the first and most important lesson I always teach:

"You are special and God loves you so much. I am so glad you are here. We are the same and God loves each of us the same—we are all His children. There are good people and bad people in every country. I pray that God brings good people into your lives, people that will encourage you and love you."

Are you the answer to that prayer? Can you provide a welcoming smile to a scared and lonely immigrant? Offer friendship and assistance? Perhaps that is your mission field ... right in your own backyard!

APPENDIX D

PROJECTING AN ATTITUDE OF WELCOMING OTHERS

In his book, *Cross-Cultural Servanthood*, Duane Elmer explores the importance of what he refers to as openness: the ability to welcome others into your presence and make them feel safe. He offers practical insights and provides illustrations from his own experiences as well as from the experiences of others.

His realistic examples help the reader to relate to his teaching, something that my husband and I experienced personally one evening regarding his discussion on openness. His example of Christians that made his wife feel like a stranger during a Bible study she was visiting (p. 41) hit uncomfortably close to home.

As an ESL teacher, I have walked into a room full of people from around the world on countless occasions and felt at ease. That night we attended a Christian financial seminar and we sat at a table next to two men who were having a discussion. The seats were placed at very close quarters and it was evident they were talking about the Old Testament and Jesus. One of them wore a large cross around his neck.

The arrangement of the table was such that my husband sat next to one of the men on one side of the table, and I sat next to the other. The chairs were less than one foot apart, yet neither of the men stopped their conversation to greet us or to even acknowledge our presence!

We sat there for a couple of minutes, and I have rarely felt that uncomfortable at a table, since the two men continued to talk as if we weren't there. My husband felt the same way and making his excuse out loud to anyone listening, he suggested we sit at another table where the view would be better. Even that did not elicit a response from the two men.

It was a relief to move to another table, and it reminded me of the story Elmer told about his wife. We felt excluded like Elmer's wife did, and in the presence of Christians. Openness is an important step if one is going to communicate the love of Christ to those around them. Elmer points out the need for us to be aware of how we are being perceived so that we can make people feel welcome and safe, not rejected.

APPENDIX E

AN IDEA YOU WON'T FIND IN MOST BOOKS ABOUT EVANGELISM

The contents of Appendix E is a discussion on an often controversial topic: the potential role of drinking in moderation when interacting with nonbelievers in social situations where alcohol is present and is NOT being abused.

This discussion encourages self-reflection, using Scripture as a guide to judicious decisions, made with discernment and emphasizing self-control.

Scripture instructs us to guard against excess, but drinking in moderation is not prohibited. Drinking alcohol may be a sin for some people and it is definitely sinful for those who abuse it, but for others who drink in moderation and responsibly, it is not necessarily a sin.

Why am I bringing this up? Because it is a scenario that has happened to my husband, Phil, and me on multiple occasions, and we have had to seek an answer to this question for ourselves.

SCENARIO 1

You stop by a neighbor's house on a Saturday afternoon to admire the car he is working on and ask if he needs any help. He says no, but it's obvious he's glad for a chance to socialize. He pulls a beer out of the cooler and offers it to you. *What do you do?*

SCENARIO 2

You and your spouse have been cultivating a relationship with the couple down the street who also have kids the same age as yours. You all decide to have a parents' night out at the local Chili's. After everyone is seated, the other couple orders a round of beer for everyone. *What do you do?*

SCENARIO 3

Your neighbor is drunk—again. He comes over to chat while you are doing yard work and it is obvious that he is slurring his words. He offers you a beer. *What do you do?*

What is really important here is that we are not talking about the behavior of a nominal Christian (one that simply warms a pew occasionally), but the behavior of a person that is truly committed to Christ, and his lifestyle and attitude towards others are a reflection of that commitment. Every situation must be considered on its own merit, by allowing the Holy Spirit to guide you in your actions.

The Apostle Paul explains his use of the freedom he has in 1 Corinthians 9:19-23. In verse 22 he writes, "I have become all things to all men so that by all possible means I might save some." If we want to reach the people around us, we will be dealing with a constant tension between secular values and biblical values.

Because the people you are desiring to reach are still under the law and have no concept of the freedom and joy to be found in Christ, they have a different perception as to what it means to be a Christian and often imagine that Christianity is simply a bunch of oppressive rules that must be followed and that you can't have any "fun" anymore.

On the other hand, abusive behavior in any form is a sin and not to be condoned. The proper response in all three scenarios is that of Christian love, but the specifics are very different. Not only must one consider the effect on your audience, but also the effect on you personally. If you have struggled with alcohol addiction in the past, your response would (and should) be very different from someone who enjoys a drink occasionally and has always enjoyed alcohol in moderation.

The reason I am bringing this up is that I have never seen it addressed in an evangelism book, yet it is a typical scenario in daily American life unless one is ensconced in a Christian bubble which prevents any opportunity to witness at all.

If we are completely honest with ourselves, while many Christians choose abstinence, many other Christians occasionally enjoy a glass of wine with dinner. I think we need to tackle these uncomfortable topics. Together, we can seek Scriptural guidance and wisdom from other mature Christians as we seek to reach the people in our Jerusalem.

When Jesus was teaching the crowds about John the Baptist and spoke of this generation, He said in Matthew 11:18-19,

> For John came neither eating nor drinking, and they say, "He has a demon." The Son of Man came eating and drinking, and they say, "Here is a glutton and a drunkard, a friend of tax collectors and 'sinners.'" But wisdom is proved right by her actions.

Matthew 11:18-19 suggests that Jesus, in befriending the lost, was being associated with their sinful habits. Gluttony is eating to excess which may be regarded as sinful, as is being a drunkard, but the context suggests that these were insults hurled at Jesus without a close look at what had actually occurred.

I can well imagine Jesus ministering to sinners while attending their dinner or party and sipping on a goblet of wine or nibbling on some snacks in the vicinity of heavier drinking and eating. But the important point (wisdom) is that He made His presence known—He hung out with them rather than condemning them, so that by His witness He was a light that they could see.

Are we so afraid of being viewed by our Christian peers as unrighteous that we won't allow ourselves to be a light in the dark by being accessible to those who need our Savior as much as we do?

In Mark 2:15-16, we learn about the ministry of Jesus and who He hung out with:

> While Jesus was having dinner at Levi's house, many tax collectors and "sinners" were eating with him and his disciples, for there were many who followed him. When the teachers of the law who were Pharisees saw him eating with the "sinners" and tax collectors, they asked

his disciples: "Why does he eat with tax collectors and 'sinners'?"

On hearing this, Jesus said to them, "It is not the healthy who need a doctor, but the sick. I have not come to call the righteous, but sinners."

If we follow the example of our Lord, we meet people where they are. Perhaps for some people, that may be over a beer occasionally, and if done with wisdom and discernment, it may just open an opportunity that would have been lost by a Pharisee ... Jesus made Himself accessible to everyone and if we do the same, then we share His heart for the lost.

CLOSING THOUGHTS

If you choose not to drink (regardless of the reason) or if your audience has obviously already indulged excessively so having a drink is not even an option to consider, your response needs to be tempered so that it is not judgmental and does not shut down a relationship that has not yet had a chance to begin.

If you think having a drink may be appropriate under the circumstances (Consider Scenarios 1 and 2), there are other things to consider including who else is present (Are there children or teens observing your behavior which could send an inappropriate message? Will your actions create a stumbling block rather than opening a door? Will there be an appropriate amount of time between consuming an alcoholic beverage and driving?).

Regardless of your position, we must remember that each of us have sins and behaviors that we struggle with and it is through the process of sanctification that we gain victory over our struggles; but this can't happen if our audience rejects the Gospel because they reject the Gospel-bringer who judges them without loving them first. This does not necessarily mean having a drink together, but it does mean being careful not to project an attitude of condemnation when offered one.

If you do not drink, or if you feel led not to accept their offer of an alcoholic beverage, "Hey, I don't really drink—but do you have a Coke? That would be great!" conveys your desire to socialize with them while allowing them to be comfortable and as a result, receptive to your offer of friendship.

APPENDIX F

I HOPE I'M GOOD ENOUGH

While visiting Phil's parents this past July, on impulse I went into a Tractor Supply store in Clovis, New Mexico to purchase some hoof conditioner for my horse back in Texas. A lady was stocking a shelf in the equine section and we began to chat.

In the course of our conversation, she mentioned that she had been studying the "end times" and felt like the rapture could happen at any time; she felt that she had messed up a lot and hoped that she was "good enough" for God to take her too.

At that moment, it broke my heart to realize the fear and daily struggle she was experiencing because she misunderstood the true nature of God's grace. If she only understood that she would never be "good enough," because if any of us could be, then we wouldn't need Jesus!

I believe it was a divine appointment that first brought me into Tractor Supply at that particular time (probably the only time I will ever be in that particular location) and then moved me to explain to a person whom I had never met before that she could never be "good enough," but that if she trusted in Jesus Christ as her Lord and Savior, that He has already prepared a place for her in heaven and she truly didn't have to worry about that anymore.

To address her concern that she still messes up, I was able to share with her that while we are saved and therefore becoming transformed to be like Christ, we still mess up and won't reach that perfection in this lifetime—but if we ask with a sorrowful heart, God forgives us and forgets our sins so that we don't have to keep holding onto the past; He is much more concerned with our present.

God tells us that it is by the blood of Jesus in His perfect sacrifice that we are forgiven of our sins and the Holy Spirit testifies to this truth in Hebrews 10:17, "Then he adds: 'Their sins and lawless acts I will remember no more.'"

The Holy Spirit prompted me to ask if I could pray for her and we stood in the horse fly spray aisle arm in arm as I prayed for her to truly know that her Savior had already assured her a place with Him in heaven. Sometimes God uses His people in order to care for His people in the most unexpected places, and that is a blessing in itself, for it gives us real joy when we know we are having an impact on others for Him and that we are furthering His kingdom—even in a Tractor Supply store!

For those of you who doubt your own salvation even though you believe that you have given your life to Jesus, I would like to remind you of what Jesus tells us in John 14:1-4:

"Do not let your hearts be troubled. Trust in God; trust also in me. In my Father's house are many rooms; if it were not so, I would have told you. I am going there to prepare a place for you. And if I go and prepare a place for you, I will come back and take you to be with me that you also may be where I am. You know the way to the place where I am going."

If you think because you mess up, God won't "take you," then consider Simon, whom Jesus gave the name "Rock," translated as Peter in Greek. In Matthew 16:18 Jesus says, "And I tell you that you are Peter, and on this rock I will build my church, and the gates of Hades will not overcome it."

Peter is like each one of us. We each have our own personal journey that we travel through life and we have our own weaknesses and fears that can paralyze our growth if we allow them to, or even cause us to do something that we really regret, like what happened to Peter when he denied Jesus. Peter was also a man of strong emotion. It wounded him to his very core that he had failed his Lord and Savior.

But God can see into our hearts and He understands our human frailties, having come to earth and experienced humanity Himself. While He led a perfect, sinless life, He surrounded Himself with humans and watched the entire spectrum of human emotion flowing around Him in the people that He loved.

We can take comfort in the fact that God understands how we feel and He forgives us when we mess up, if we respond to our sin like Peter did, heartbroken and repentant. And that like Peter, God will use even us ordinary folk to take care of His sheep if we will but follow Him. We can't love perfectly like Jesus can, but we can love as He calls us to. And like Peter, if it is our all, it will be enough.

There are many Scriptures that can bring you assurance in your eternal security:

The Apostle Paul writes in Romans 7:14-24 of his own struggle with sin,

> We know that the law is spiritual; but I am unspiritual, sold as a slave to sin. I do not understand what I do. For

what I want to do I do not do, but what I hate I do. And if I do what I do not want to do, I agree that the law is good. As it is, it is no longer I myself who do it, but it is sin living in me. I know that nothing good lives in me, that is, in my sinful nature. For I have the desire to do what is good, but I cannot carry it out. For what I do is not the good I want to do; no, the evil I do not want to do —this I keep on doing. Now if I do what I do not want to do, it is no longer I who do it, but it is sin living in me that does it.

So I find this law at work: When I want to do good, evil is right there with me. For in my inner being I delight in God's law; but I see another law at work in the members of my body, waging war against the law of my mind and making me a prisoner of the law of sin at work within my members. What a wretched man I am! Who will rescue me from this body of death?

But take note of our deliverance in verse 25: "Thanks be to God —through Jesus Christ our Lord!"

Paul also writes to us in Romans 8:38-39 regarding the love of God,

For I am convinced that neither death nor life, neither angels nor demons, neither the present nor the future, nor any powers, neither height nor depth, nor anything else in all creation, will be able to separate us from the love of God that is in Christ Jesus our Lord.

Jesus tells us in John 10:27-30,

My sheep listen to my voice; I know them, and they follow me. I give them eternal life, and they shall never perish; no one can snatch them out of my hand. My Father, who has given them to me, is greater than all; no one can snatch them out of my Father's hand. I and the Father are one.

In Ephesians 1:13-14 we learn:

And you also were included in Christ when you heard the word of truth, the gospel of your salvation. Having believed, you were marked in him with a seal, the promised Holy Spirit, who is a deposit guaranteeing our inheritance until the redemption of those who are God's possession—to the praise of his glory.

One of my favorite books in the Bible is 1 John because it offers Christians great assurance in their salvation. John even shares his reason for writing in 1 John 5:13,

I write these things to you who believe in the name of the Son of God so that you may know that you have eternal life.

Rest assured, my Christian brothers and sisters, that by Romans 10:9, "That if you confess with your mouth, 'Jesus is Lord,' and believe in your heart that God raised him from the dead, you will be saved." The work that Jesus did on the cross completely covers all of our transgressions—past, present and future.

We can never be good enough on our own—never—but we can have full confidence in Romans 8:1, "Therefore, there is now no condemnation for those who are in Christ Jesus," *and it is truly in Him alone that we are good enough!*

APPENDIX G

SKILLS TO DEVELOP FOR SUCCESSFUL COMMUNICATION

1. *Most importantly, learn to develop a dependence on the Holy Spirit. It takes the pressure off and lets Him work through you, instead of you getting in His way.*
2. *Be a good listener. I can't emphasis this skill enough. Have you ever caught yourself only half-listening because you are thinking about what you want to say? I have and it only creates an obstacle. Remember that it's not about you —it's about the person in front of you who needs Christ.*
3. *Don't try to force the conversation; just talk about what comes naturally.*
4. *Ask questions that invite your friends to express themselves or to share stories.*
5. *Be aware of body language and respond appropriately. You can often tell more about how a person is feeling through observation than words.*
6. *A smile goes a long way. Be humble, gracious, and welcoming. You don't have to know everything; you just have to love people. They will become receptive when they know your love is genuine.*

7. *Be discerning. Often a person will give you an opening that leads naturally to spiritual matters.*

8. *Also be discerning as to when to exit a discussion about spiritual matters so that your friend has time to absorb what you are sharing without feeling pressured.*

9. *End conversations on a positive note, if possible, and suggest making plans to meet again soon. If you are comfortable and feel led, ask your friend if you can pray for them before you go.*

10. *When having a conversation with someone who is obviously looking for an argument, don't enter the battle and try to prove your position. Chances are the person may have had this same conversation one hundred times before and simply enjoys debating why he or she shouldn't believe. Most of these folks have not only studied scientific theories and philosophy, but also know the Bible better than most Christians. Your best course of action is to appeal to their emotions because they have already decided what they believe by logic. Just be their friend and let your own life be a witness.*

11. *Email, Facebook, texting, and phone calls are great tools for keeping in touch without being overbearing. Drop your friend a line in a few days stating how much you enjoyed your visit and that you were just wondering how they are doing.*

APPENDIX H

TO MY FRIENDS OF ALL FAITHS AND THOSE WITH NO PARTICULAR FAITH

This letter has been many years in coming. It is a hard letter for me to write, because I love all of you so much, and I would never want to offend you. But I feel compelled to write these words because of that love – I want to see you in heaven.

If you know me, you know I have always been respectful of those who hold different beliefs than me. I have been so blessed to have made friends from many different countries, and the most joyful times of my life have been getting to know people from cultures very different from my own.

Anyone who knows me also knows I am a Christian. I do not take my commitment to being a Christian casually. While I am not always successful, I do my best to live according to God's instructions in the Bible. In the words of C.S. Lewis, "I believe in Christianity as I believe that the sun has risen: not only because I see it, but because by it I see everything else." My hope and desire is that my daily actions reflect the love of Christ to those around me.

Some important things to know about Christianity:

A Christian believes that the Bible is the inerrant Word of

God. In other words, whatever it says has come from God and is true. What I read in the Bible, I can trust.

God loves EVERYONE. Really, it's true! It doesn't matter what you have done in the past – you can't change the fact that God loves you and He wants to have a relationship with you – that is why He created you!

If you are worried because you have done bad things, sadly, we all have. This is called sin, and it separates us from God because He is holy and without sin. But the good news is, no one is so far from God that they can't be forgiven and enter into His family. God's love is unconditional.

It's important to know that God's grace is offered to all, but He gives us a choice. The only requirement is for a person to choose to accept it by believing in His Son, that Jesus came to Earth, died for our sins (taking the penalty of sin in our place), and was raised from the dead—giving victory over death and a place in heaven for those who believe in Him. If you do, your life will never be the same! You will have entered into a personal relationship with the Creator of the universe.

Our God is a God of relationship. He wants to have conversations with you. He wants you to depend on Him. He is always available to you. In fact, His Holy Spirit provides both guidance and comfort to those who believe. The Holy Spirit also convicts us and helps us live a life pleasing to God. It's mind-boggling, I know. It's hard to comprehend, but it's true!

We read in the Bible in John 14:6: **Jesus answered, "I am the way, the truth, and the life. No one can come to the Father except through me."**

From a Christian perspective, one **must** have a personal relationship with Jesus in order to "come to the Father" and gain entrance into heaven. In order to do that, they must ask Jesus to be their Lord and Savior, and trust in Him for their salvation.

Thus, my dilemma. I believe that in order to have salvation, one must accept the same things I believe, even if you come from a different country and/or were raised in another religion or no religion at all. Even if you try to be a good person, no other religion meets this requirement, and no one is good enough to get into heaven by their own efforts.

Salvation is a free gift, but a person must choose to accept it and place their faith in Jesus. *Knowing I believe this, if I am truly your friend and I love you like I say I do, I must be concerned about your eternal destiny. How can I not share this with you?*

Putting myself in your shoes – my first reaction might be – how unfair! How exclusive! Why can't all paths lead to heaven? Why does a Christian think they are better than everybody else?

My answer to the last question starts us on our journey: A true Christian KNOWS they are no better than anyone else. It is the same desperate need that we all have to be cleansed from our sins that make us all equally in need of a Savior. Sin separates us from God.

We can't fix our situation – only Jesus can by taking the penalty of our sins for us. Jesus offers to do that for each and every one of us. No other path provides the atonement required to satisfy God's wrath (His holy standard) because of our sins. No other way forms a bridge over the yawning chasm of our sins so that we can enjoy God's presence for eternity.

While the entrance to heaven is exclusively for those who call upon the Name of Jesus, accepting Him as both the Lord over their life and their Savior, Christianity is far from exclusive. God wants EVERYONE to be reconciled to Him. It doesn't matter where you are from, what your cultural background is, what color you are, or what language you speak; ALL are welcome.

Does this seem unfair? I personally am grateful to Jesus that I am not treated fairly, because if I were, I would have to suffer for my sins. I am grateful that God so loved the world that He created a way for us to enter heaven by being merciful instead of fair: He sent His only Son to die for us in our place.

In the Bible, John 3:16-17 says, "For God so loved THE WORLD, that He gave His one and only Son, that whoever believes in him shall not perish but have eternal life. For God did not send his Son into the world to condemn the world, but that the world might be saved through him." THE WORLD – all of us!

I can tell you about my own relationship with Jesus – how He has changed everything in my life for the better and, even now, walks alongside me, comforting and helping me through my greatest trials. How He is faithful even when I'm not, and He loves me despite all of my sins. I also know I am going to Heaven with certainty, because I have placed my trust in Him.

When I expressed my concern to a dear friend of mine who is Muslim, regarding his eternal destiny, he responded: "Perhaps God will open my heart to Jesus. It is up to Him." His words were so wise!

That reminded me that I am not the one who can convince you about who Jesus is and the grace that He offers each one of us; that is up to the Holy Spirit to move in your heart. It is my prayer that He is moving, even now. I love you.

If you have read this and I managed to offend you, I am truly sorry. But from my perspective, your eternal life is at stake. If I truly love you, I have to at least try to share this with you. If you are curious and have questions, I would be glad to answer them, and if I don't know, I will find out. Whatever you choose, ultimately, the decision is yours, and regardless, I will always be your friend. Thank you for allowing me to share my heart with you.

If you find yourself wanting to learn more – the video below is an amazing message because it teaches us about the incredible, extravagant, and incomparable love God has for us, and it also explains the cross – something that puzzles many people. If you have ever wondered why the Son of God would allow Himself to be crucified on a cross – this is a great sermon to listen to. Spoiler Alert: It has everything to do with God's love for us!

God tells us in Jeremiah 29:13, "You will seek me and find me when you seek me with all your heart." My prayer for you is that you find God and rest in His extravagant love for you. Amen

You can find this blog post with the video at:
https://novelwrites.com/2021/02/21/to-my-friends-of-all-faiths-and-those-with-no-particular-faith/

APPENDIX I

SUGGESTED READING LIST

1. Cross-Cultural Servanthood: Serving the World in Christlike Humility by Duane Elmer

This is one of my favorite books because you can't help but be struck by the humility of the author. He shares real-life examples and often hits upon truths that have had a profound effect on how I see both myself and others. Elmer brings us a little closer to seeing through the lens of Jesus and does it in a way that is fun and easy to read.

2. Share Jesus Without Fear by William Fay and Linda Evans Shepherd

I really like the way Fay provides answers to many of the questions that a seeker may have, as well as ways to respond to their possible objections. As I mentioned earlier, I don't typically follow Fay's single encounter approach, but his systematic way of presenting Scripture gives me a framework that I sometimes use when witnessing that I am comfortable with.

3. The Art of Personal Evangelism: Sharing Jesus in a Changing Culture by Will McRaney

This is a great book for digging a little deeper. McRaney gives us lots of insight into postmodern culture and great tips on communication. He also devotes a lot of effort towards overcoming barriers to following Christ.

4. *Conspiracy of Kindness* by Steve Sjogren

This book offers lots of innovative ideas for doing service evangelism.

5. *Evangelism Is--: How to Share Jesus With Passion and Confidence* by Dave Wheeler and David Earley

Wheeler and Earley do a great job giving inspiration and direction in an easy-to-read format.

Be sure and check out the books in the Bibliography section for additional resources.

EPILOGUE

You may recall that in Chapter 5, Creating a Relational Approach to Evangelism that is Right for You, I mention my friend in the section on "Suggestions for Loving Your Neighbor," and more specifically, in the topic, *Don't Set Any Agendas*. In Chapter 6, The Fundamentals, I also mentioned sharing the Gospel with her in "My Favorite Gospel Illustration on a Napkin."

PAUL TELLS us in 1 Corinthians 3:6-7,

> I planted the seed, Apollos watered it, but God has been making it grow. So neither the one who plants nor the one who waters is anything, but only God, who makes things grow.

We can interpret from this verse that while we may have a part in a person's journey to salvation, the results belong to the Lord, and we may never know if we have had an impact on pointing a person to Christ. Our job is to be obedient and respond as the Holy Spirit leads – trusting in Him for whatever happens, no matter how far off into the future or if we are around to get to see it.

But sometimes, we do get to experience the joy of seeing what happens!

Recall Appendix A, where you read about my mother coming to understand that Jesus is the Messiah she was waiting for. My dear mother went to be with her Lord and Savior a few years ago. It was very hard to say goodbye, but my comfort is in knowing she is with Jesus, and one day, we will be reunited again.

My friend from Chapter 5 came to my mother's memorial service to honor our friendship. I was truly touched but was unaware of the amazing and wonderful thing that was about to happen. We had asked the pastor conducting mom's memorial service to please make sure and do an altar call – in other words, as part of the service, talk about the salvation that can be found in Jesus Christ.

The pastor read many Scriptures that spoke to what Jesus did for us, and His gift of grace that was freely available to all. As the service ended, my friend came up to me. I'll never forget the words she spoke as tears rolled down her cheeks and the look of profound joy on her face, "I know I'll never be alone again."

NOTES

ALL SCRIPTURAL REFERENCES ARE FROM THE
NEW INTERNATIONAL VERSION

1. Tim Dearborn, "Beyond Duty", in *Perspectives on the World Christian Movement: A Reader*, 3rd edition, eds. Ralph D. Winter and Steven C. Hawthorne (Pasadena: William Carey Library, 2009), 70.

2. Henry T. Blackaby and Avery T. Willis, Jr., "On Mission With God", in *Perspectives on the World Christian Movement: A Reader*, 3rd edition, eds. Ralph D. Winter and Steven C. Hawthorne (Pasadena: William Carey Library, 2009), 77.

3. C. Hawthorne, "The Story of His Glory", in *Perspectives on the World Christian Movement: A Reader*, 3rd edition, eds. Ralph D. Winter and Steven C. Hawthorne (Pasadena: William Carey Library, 2009), 51.

4. A. Scott Moreau, Gary R. Corwin and Gary B. McGee, *Introducing World Missions: a Biblical, Historical, and Practical Survey* (Grand Rapids, Mich.: Baker Academic, 2004), 31.

5. Sarita D. Gallagher and Steven C. Hawthorne, "Blessing as Transformation", in *Perspectives on*

the World Christian Movement: A Reader, 3rd edition, eds. Ralph D. Winter and Steven C. Hawthorne (Pasadena: William Carey Library, 2009), 37-38.

6. Moreau, Corwin and McGee, *Introducing World Missions*, 32.

7. George Eldon Ladd, "The Gospel of the Kingdom", in *Perspectives on the World Christian Movement: A Reader*, 3rd edition, eds. Ralph D. Winter and Steven C. Hawthorne (Pasadena: William Carey Library, 2009), 88.

8. Steven C. Hawthorne, "The Story of His Glory", in *Perspectives on the World Christian Movement: A Reader*, 3rd edition, eds. Ralph D. Winter and Steven C. Hawthorne (Pasadena: William Carey Library, 2009), 51.

9. Moreau, Corwin and McGee, *Introducing World Missions*, 79-85.

10. Dean Flemming, *Contextualization in the New Testament: Patterns For Theology and Mission* (Downers Grove: IVP Academic, 2005), 72.

11. Blackaby and Willis, Jr., "On Mission With God," 77.

12. Ladd, "The Gospel of the Kingdom," 88.

13. Dave Earley & David Wheeler, *Evangelism Is--: How to Share Jesus with Passion and Confidence* (Nashville: B&H Academic, 2010), 196-197.

14. Ibid., 50.

15. Paul G. Hiebert, *The Gospel in the Context of Modernity* (Lectures at Abilene Christian University, May 25, 2004).

16. Moreau, Corwin and McGee, *Introducing World Missions*, 268.

17. Ibid., 268-269.

18. Lausanne Occasional Paper 2: *The Willowbank Report: Consultation on Gospel and Culture* (Lausanne Committee for World Evangelization, 1978), 2.

19. Duane Elmer, *Cross-Cultural Servanthood: Serving the World in Christlike Humility* (Downers Grove: IVP Books, 2006), 27-28.

20. David J. Hesselgrave, "The Role of Culture in Communication", in *Perspectives on the World Christian Movement: A Reader*, 3rd edition, eds. Ralph D. Winter and Steven C. Hawthorne (Pasadena: William Carey Library, 2009), 428.

21. William Fay with Linda Evans Shepherd, *Share Jesus Without Fear* (Nashville: B&H Publishing Group, 1999), general reference.

22. Steve Sjogren, *Conspiracy of Kindness, A Refreshing New Approach to Sharing the Love of Jesus* (Ventura: Regal Books, 2003), back cover.

23. Dallas Willard, *Conspiracy of Kindness, A Refreshing New Approach to Sharing the Love of Jesus* (Ventura: Regal Books, 2003), back cover.

24. Sjogren, *Conspiracy of Kindness,* 31.

25. Ibid., 22.

26. Ibid., 26.

27. Ibid., 221,230.

28. Ibid., 31.

29. Keith E. Swartley, "Our Response to Islam: Introduction," in *Encountering the World of Islam,* ed. Keith E. Swartley (Waynesboro: Authentic Media, 2005), 403.

30. Earley & Wheeler, *Evangelism Is ...,* 200.

31. Will McRaney and Jr, *The Art of Personal Evangelism: Sharing Jesus in a Changing Culture* (Nashville: B&H Academic, 2003), 110.

32. Carl Medearis, *Muslims, Christians, and Jesus: Gaining Understandings and Building Relationships* (Minneapolis: Bethany House Publishers, 2008), 178-179.

33. David Earley, *Presentation on Evangelism* (Online Video Lecture at Liberty Baptist Theological Seminary for EVAN 565, Fall 2011).

34. Napkin illustration is not the author's original idea, it is a modified version excerpted from *Becoming a Contagious Christian* by Bill Hybels and Mark Mittelberg adapted from "The Bridge" @1981 by The Navigators.

35. Originally read on an email that was circulating the internet, author unknown.

36. Fay, *Share Jesus Without Fear,* 192.

37. Ibid., 192.

38. Earley & Wheeler, *Evangelism Is ...,* 99.

39. Ibid., 72.

40. Ibid., 73.

41. Ibid., 99.

BIBLIOGRAPHY

Barker, Kenneth, ed. *New International Version Study Bible*. Grand Rapids: Zondervan, 2002.

Blackaby, Henry T., and Avery T. Willis, Jr. "On Mission With God." In *Perspectives on the World Christian Movement: A Reader*, 3rd edition, edited by Ralph D. Winter and Steven C. Hawthorne, 74-77. Pasadena: William Carey Library, 2009.

Dearborn, Tim. "Beyond Duty." In *Perspectives on the World Christian Movement: A Reader*, 3rd edition, edited by Ralph D. Winter and Steven C. Hawthorne, 70-73. Pasadena: William Carey Library, 2009.

Elmer, Duane. *Cross-Cultural Servanthood: Serving the World in Christlike Humility*. Downers Grove: IVP Books, 2006.

Fay, William, and Linda Evans Shepherd. *Share Jesus Without Fear*. Nashville: B&H Publishing Group, 1999.

Flemming, Dean. *Contextualization in the New Testament: Patterns For Theology and Mission*. Downers Grove: IVP Academic, 2005.

Gallagher, Sarita D., and Steven C. Hawthorne. "Blessing as Transformation." In *Perspectives on the World Christian Movement: A Reader*, 3rd edition, edited by Ralph D. Winter and Steven C. Hawthorne, 34-41. Pasadena: William Carey Library, 2009.

Hawthorne, Steven C. "The Story of His Glory." In *Perspectives on the World Christian Movement: A Reader*, 3rd edition, edited by Ralph D. Winter and Steven C. Hawthorne, 49-63. Pasadena: William Carey Library, 2009.

Hesselgrave, David J. "The Role of Culture in Communication." In *Perspectives on the World Christian Movement: A Reader*, 3rd edition, edited by Ralph D. Winter and Steven C. Hawthorne, 425-429. Pasadena: William Carey Library, 2009.

Ladd, George Eldon. "The Gospel of the Kingdom." In *Perspectives on the World Christian Movement: A Reader*, 3rd edition, edited by Ralph D. Winter and Steven C. Hawthorne, 83-95. Pasadena: William Carey Library, 2009.

Lausanne Occasional Paper 2. "The Willowbank Report: Consultation on Gospel and Culture." Lausanne Committee for World Evangelization, 1978.

McRaney, Will, and Jr. *The Art of Personal Evangelism: Sharing Jesus in a Changing Culture*. Nashville: B&H Academic, 2003.

Medearis, Carl. *Muslims, Christians, and Jesus: Gaining Understandings and Building Relationships*. Minneapolis: Bethany House Publishers, 2008.

Moreau, A. Scott, Gary R. Corwin, and Gary B. McGee. *Introducing World Missions: a Biblical, Historical, and Practical Survey*. Grand Rapids: Baker Academic, 2004.

Sjogren, Steve. *Conspiracy of Kindness, A Refreshing New Approach to Sharing the Love of Jesus*. Ventura: Regal Books, 2003.

Swartley, Keith E. "Past Approaches To Outreach: Introduction." In *Encountering the World of Islam*, edited by Keith E. Swartley, 311-313. Waynesboro: Authentic Media, 2005.

Tennent, Timothy C. *Theology in the Context of World Christianity*. Grand Rapids: Zondervan, 2007.

Wheeler, Dave and David Earley. *Evangelism Is--: How to Share Jesus with Passion and Confidence*. Nashville: B&H Academic, 2010.

BENEDICTION

May you move through each day open to the opportunities that the Holy Spirit provides you to share God's love with others. May you respond naturally and joyfully, knowing God is using you to bring others to Himself through His Son, Jesus Christ, so that they, too, can experience His mercy and grace! Live in the blessed assurance of salvation Jesus provides to those who call upon Him as Lord and Savior. Be a light in the darkness, love one another, and be forgiving of one another as Christ forgives us. Go in peace.

Amen

TAKING BACK BIBLE STUDY
COMING 2025

Taking Back Bible Study: Moving Deeper into the Word of God

If you are like me, you may have read the Bible for many years. You may have even read through it, maybe more than once.

Before I learned the simple three-step method, often referred to as Inductive Bible Study, I had no idea how to dig deeper into the meaning of what I was reading. The biblical audience lived in a different world with a different culture and a different worldview. How could I gain a deeper understanding of Scripture without depending on others to explain it for me?

My class on How to Study the Bible at Dallas Christian College changed everything. I learned how to study Scripture in such a way that still depended on the Holy Spirit but explored the meaning of the text in the context it was written, and how to (being faithful to the original text) bring it forward to how I can apply it to my own life.

Since then, many of my friends who have been in church for years have expressed the desire to be able to do the same. They were all very familiar with Scripture but had never been taught how to dig deeper. I'll never forget the excitement of one of my students when taking a class I was teaching on How to Study the Bible.

When it came time to choose a passage to focus on—while learning the principles of the course—she was very excited to share that she had chosen a passage that had bothered her for years. She desperately wanted clarity on it. By the end of the course, she had done the necessary interpretive work using the principles of Inductive Bible Study and was able to come to a place of both understanding and peace because of the new skills in Bible Study she had learned.

In the pages of this book, you'll learn how to study the Bible in ways that are both comfortable for you and effective. Since it is all about learning how to dig deeper into understanding God's Word, you will be excited and blessed as you begin to implement what you learn, with plenty of examples and encouragement along the way.

You won't find a huge, scholarly tome here – but an easy-to-read book that is intentionally not very long. We think you will find it very convenient to fit this study into even the busiest of schedules and still gain the tools you need to approach Bible Study with joy and confidence.

Taking Back Bible Study lends itself well to a group study, but it can also be read individually at a more rapid pace or adjusted to fit into a seminar format. The discussion questions and exercises are designed to help you build a strong foundation. By the end of the book, you will have completed your very own detailed interpretation of a Scripture passage you have chosen for yourself, and you will have acquired the necessary skills to move deeper into God's Word.

An online class for Taking Back Bible Study is also in the works and will be offered for both individuals and small groups. Check nancy-golden.com frequently for updates.

ACKNOWLEDGMENTS

I am so grateful to my Lord and Savior, Jesus Christ, for this opportunity to use my gifts for kingdom work and, most of all, for the work He did at the cross, which gives this book its purpose.

The writing journey can be arduous at times, and having people in an author's life to support and offer encouragement is often the tipping point for the successful completion of a book. Taking Back the Gospel is no exception. The faithful cast of characters that have helped me on my writing journey include, first and foremost, my Lord and Savior, Jesus Christ, who gives me strength to keep going.

Next comes my incredible husband, whose love and support make it possible for me to sit in front of a computer for hours as I seek to put words to paper. He shares my dream of having a positive impact on others through the writing gifts God has blessed me with, and I am grateful more than I can ever express.

My son Josh and his beautiful wife Naomi never fail to be an encouragement and—on occasion—a part of my projects. I am excited to share that Naomi is a very talented graphic artist. She has used her amazing creativity to create the cover for *Taking Back the Gospel*. I couldn't be more delighted with her work. You can find her at naomigoldencreative.com

Thanks also to my wonderful colleagues at Dallas Christian College; they are a remarkable group of dedicated educators, and over the years, they have blessed me richly with their wisdom and their friendship.

Heartfelt thanks to Pastor Chad and Jennifer Burton of Living Word Global Church; their enthusiasm for this project helped me keep my momentum as I persevered to finish the race. Truly, you are meeting Jesus when you meet this precious couple.

Thanks also to my editors, Jason Harrell and Joseph Frederickson. They generously shared their command of the English language with this project. I would also like to thank my "horse" buddy, Cathy Buchanan, who kindly read the manuscript and contributed to the final edits, and in special remembrance of her husband, Barry Buchanan, who leaves a legacy of Second Greatest Commandment love that inspires all of us.

A special thanks to Larry Luby, who offered the wisdom and encouragement I needed regarding the practical aspects of publishing a book while offering spiritual insights along the way.

And, of course, I can't forget to mention my wonderful mother, Leah Venetucci, because "the apple doesn't fall far from the tree."

This book was also inspired by the loving memory of Joshua Hernandez, who went to be with the Lord sooner than any of us were ready for. He is with the Lord now, thanks to someone caring enough to share the Gospel with him—an inspiration for all of us to go forth and share our faith, because each day is a precious gift, and every one of us is in need of our Savior.

POSTSCRIPT

I hope the contents of this book has given you a strong foundation you can draw from to share your faith, in ways natural to your own style of evangelism while following the leading of the Holy Spirit. If it has, please recommend Taking Back the Gospel to your family and friends.

Being an author is hard work, but it's also a joy. My heart's desire is for the words I write to have a positive impact on you. If you enjoyed this book or have any questions and/or feedback, I would love to hear from you. You can email me directly with your comments at nancy@goldencrossranch.com

One of the very best things you can do for an author is to leave a review on Amazon and/or Goodreads – I hope you'll consider doing so.

May the grace and peace of our Lord Jesus Christ be with you always,
Nancy Golden

ABOUT THE AUTHOR

Nancy Golden graduated from Dallas Christian College and earned her master's degree (MAR) from Liberty Baptist Theological Seminary. She is an adjunct faculty member at Dallas Christian College and an instructor for <u>BeADisciple.com</u>.

Her seminary work includes Theology, Bible, and Intercultural Studies in Religion. Nancy and her husband, Phil, are members of Living Word Global Church in Irving, Texas. She is an avid horsewoman and loves to sing praise and worship songs when she is riding.

Writing across several genres, Nancy focuses on entertaining, clean, uplifting fiction and non-fiction. Visit her author website at https://nancy-golden.com to learn more about her writing projects and read her ramblings about this journey called life.

You can also email any comments you may have to nancy@goldencrossranch.com - *Nancy would love to hear from you!*

ALSO BY NANCY GOLDEN

Taking Back Advent

Alien Neighbors

Sword of Fate

Taking Back Lent